The **AA** **POCKET**Guide

# DISNEYLAND®

# RESORT

# PARIS

**Original text by Lindsay Hunt**

Updated by Lindsay Hunt

© Automobile Association Developments Limited 2008
First published 2008

ISBN: 978-0-7495-5509-2

Published by AA Publishing, a trading name of Automobile Association Developments
Limited, whose registered office is Fanum House, Basing View, Basingstoke,
Hampshire RG21 4EA. Registered number 1878835.

A CIP catalogue record for this book is available from the British Library

Colour separation: Keenes, Andover
Printed and bound in Italy by Printer Trento S.r.l.

Front and back cover images © Disney

A03404

# About this book

**Symbols are used to denote the following categories:**

- ✉ address or location
- ☎ telephone number
- 🕐 opening times
- ✋ admission charge
- 🍴 restaurant or café on premises or nearby
- Ⓜ nearest underground train station
- 🚌 nearest bus/tram route
- 🚆 nearest overground train station
- ⛴ nearest ferry stop
- ✈ nearest airport
- ↔ other places of interest nearby
- ❓ other practical information
- ➤ indicates the page where you will find a fuller description

This book is divided into five sections.

# Contents

# EXCURSIONS

# PARIS

# INDEX & ACKNOWLEDGEMENTS

# Planning

© Disney

# Before You Go

## WHEN TO GO

| JAN | FEB | MAR | APR | MAY | JUN | JUL | AUG | SEP | OCT | NOV | DEC |
|---|---|---|---|---|---|---|---|---|---|---|---|
| 7°C | 7°C | 10°C | 16°C | 17°C | 23°C | 25°C | 26°C | 21°C | 16°C | 12°C | 8°C |
| 45°F | 45°F | 50°F | 61°F | 63°F | 73°F | 77°F | 79°F | 70°F | 61°F | 54°F | 46°F |

High season  Low season

Marne-la-Vallée's climate is rather drier than that of coastal France. The wettest months are from November to January and from March to May (all have more than 15 days of rainfall—not necessarily, of course, all day long). Highest temperatures are predictably in July and August, when a sunhat is advisable. Between May and June and September and October there are pleasantly equable temperatures, and daytime highs are between 16°C and 21°C (61°C and 70°F). Otherwise, it is unusual to experience climatic extremes or sharp seasonal variations. Average temperatures stay above freezing all year round, and it rarely gets too hot to stay outside in the middle of the day.

## WHAT YOU NEED

● Required
○ Suggested
▲ Not required

Some countries require a passport to remain valid for a minimum period (usually at least six months) beyond the date of entry – check before you travel.

| | UK | Germany | USA | Canada | Australia | Ireland | Netherlands | Spain |
|---|---|---|---|---|---|---|---|---|
| Passport (or National Identity Card where applicable) | ● | ● | ● | ● | ● | ● | ● | ● |
| Visa (regulations can change – check before you travel) | ▲ | ▲ | ▲ | ▲ | ▲ | ▲ | ▲ | ▲ |
| Onward or Return Ticket | ▲ | ▲ | ▲ | ▲ | ▲ | ▲ | ▲ | ▲ |
| Health Inoculations (tetanus and polio) | ▲ | ▲ | ▲ | ▲ | ▲ | ▲ | ▲ | ▲ |
| Health Documentation (▶ 9, Health Advice) | ● | ● | ● | ● | ● | ● | ● | ● |
| Travel Insurance | ○ | ○ | ○ | ○ | ○ | ○ | ○ | ○ |
| Driving Licence (national) | ● | ● | ● | ● | ● | ● | ● | ● |
| Car Insurance Certificate | ○ | ○ | n/a | n/a | n/a | ○ | ○ | ○ |
| Car Registration Document | ● | ● | n/a | n/a | n/a | ● | ● | ● |

## TOURIST OFFICES AT HOME

### Maison de la France

### In the UK
178 Piccadilly,
London W1J 9AL
☎ 09068 244123;
fax: 202 7493 6594

### In the USA
444 Madison Avenue, 16th floor,
New York NY10022
☎ 410/286 8310;
fax: 212/838 7855

9454 Wilshire Boulevard,
Suite 715, Beverly Hills CA90212
☎ 310/271 6665;
fax: 310/276 2835

## HEALTH ADVICE
### Insurance
Nationals of EU countries can obtain medical treatment at reduced cost in France with a European Health Insurance Card (EHIC), available from the Post Office, although private medical insurance is still advised and is essential for all other visitors.

### Medical treatment
Minor ailments can often be treated at pharmacies. All public hospitals have a 24-hour emergency service *(urgences)* as well as specialist doctors. Payment is made on the spot, but if you are hospitalized ask to see the *assistante sociale* to arrange payment directly through your insurance.

### Dental services
As for general medical treatment, nationals of EU countries can obtain dental treatment at reduced cost. Around 70 per cent of standard dentists' fees are refunded.

## TIME DIFFERENCES

| GMT | France | Spain | USA (NY) | USA (West Coast) | Sydney |
|---|---|---|---|---|---|
| 12 noon | 1PM | 1PM | 7AM | 4AM | 10PM |

France is on Central European Time (GMT+1). From late March, when clocks are put forward one hour, until late October, French summer time (GMT+2) operates.

## DATES TO AVOID

You may be tied to school holiday times, but to avoid crowds, try to miss popular French holidays (▶ 13). You can also expect more crowds around Easter and Whitsuntide. French school holidays are staggered, lasting several weeks (mid-April to mid-May; early July to early September). August is a traditional holiday month for many Parisians who may well visit Disneyland® Resort Paris then.

## RESERVATIONS AND ADVANCE PLANNING

To reserve accommodation or to rent cars at Disneyland Resort

© Disney

Paris, call Reservations on 08705 03 03 03 (national rate call), seven days a week. From Eire, dial 00331 60 30 60 53 (international rate call) from Monday to Friday 8am– 8pm, Saturday 9am– 6pm (5pm on Sunday). Park times vary so please check with the Disneyland Resort Paris website.
www.disneylandparis.co.uk or www.disneylandparis.com for more information. Inside France, call ☎ 01 60 30 60 30.

## TIGHT BUDGET

Taking a family to Disneyland Resort Paris is by no means a budget option but there are ways to cut the costs.

● All those ice-creams, soft drinks, T-shirts and mouse ears soon mount up to a hefty bill. Resist too many impulse buys.

● Choose counter-service cafés or food cart snacks rather than the more expensive table-service restaurants. Or bring a picnic to the picnic area between guest parking and the Disney® Parks.

● Families and friends can save money by sharing a room – all the Disney® Hotels have rooms suitable for parties of four (Disney's Davy Crockett Ranch® 2-bedroom log cabins sleep six and Disney's Newport Bay Club® has rooms that can accommodate six people).

● You can stay at one of the many non-Disney hotels scattered around the resort, or even in central Paris.

● Buying two separate 1-day Park tickets and spending a day in each Park might save a few euros on the current cost of a 2-Day Hopper, but the best-value option for most visitors is a 3-Day Hopper, allowing free movement between both Parks within the allotted time frame. You don't have to use your ticket on consecutive days; tickets remain valid for 1 year from the date on the back of the ticket.

● Take some light rainwear to avoid buying Mickey Mouse ponchos or umbrellas if it rains.

● Try to avoid the expensive video games arcades.

## WHAT'S ON WHEN

### DISNEYLAND® RESORT PARIS

Besides the big parades that take place daily, or whenever Disneyland® Park is open late, special holidays are marked by extra-spectacular extravaganzas. New Year witnesses even more fireworks than usual and parties in all the hotels. Special parades are held periodically throughout the year. Needless to say, Christmas is celebrated with carols and a tree. Other events are planned at shorter notice during the year.

© Disney

### PARIS

#### January/February

*Le Grande Parade de Paris:* The Parisian New Year festival takes place in different venues around the city (www.parisparade.com).
*Chinese New Year:* Dragon parades and other Oriental festivities in Chinatown.

#### March/April

*Marathon International de Paris:* Starting from place de la Concorde and finishing on avenue Foch behind the Arc de Triomphe.

#### April/May

*International Paris Fair:* Food, homes and gardens and much more at Porte de Versailles.

#### May–June

*Labour Day* (1 May): Processions.
*Paris Jazz Festival:* Free concerts on summer weekend afternoons.
*Festival Foire Saint-Germain* (Jun): Village traditions revived.
*Fête de la Musique* (21 Jun): Everything from classical to techno, both indoors and out.

#### July–August

*Bastille Day* (14 Jul): This highly significant date is celebrated with fireworks and street dances on the evening of the 13th and a parade on the 14th on the Champs-Élysées.
*Paris, Quartier d'Eté:* Open-air music, plays and dance.

## NATIONAL HOLIDAYS

| JAN | FEB | MAR | APR | MAY | JUN | JUL | AUG | SEP | OCT | NOV | DEC |
|-----|-----|-----|-----|-----|-----|-----|-----|-----|-----|-----|-----|
| 1 | | (1) | (1) | 2(2) | (1) | 1 | 1 | | | 2 | 1 |

| | |
|---|---|
| **1 Jan** | New Year's Day |
| **Mar/Apr** | Easter Sunday and Monday |
| **1 May** | Labour Day |
| **May** | Ascension Day |
| **May/Jun** | Whit Sunday and Monday |
| **14 Jul** | Bastille Day |
| **15 Aug** | Assumption Day |
| **1 Nov** | All Saints' Day |
| **11 Nov** | Remembrance Day |
| **25 Dec** | Christmas Day |

Banks, businesses, museums and most shops (except boulangeries) are closed on these days, but this does not apply to Disneyland® Resort Paris.

*Fête des Tuileries:* Jardin des Tuileries becomes a fairground (begins end of June).

### September
*Festival d'Automne O* (mid Sep–end Dec): Music, theatre and dance throughout the city.

### October
*Faire Internationale d'Art Contemporain:* Paris's biggest modern art fair, at the Pavillon du Parc, Paris Expo, Porte de Versailles.

### December
*Salon Nautique International:* International boat show at the Porte de Versailles.

### OTHER OPTIONS
Many places within easy reach of Disneyland Resort Paris hold special events.
**Meaux** has a summer festival with *son et lumière* shows in the grounds of the Bishop's Palace.
**Reims** celebrates when champagne grapes are harvested.
**Versailles** puts on grand fountain shows in summer.
At **Fontainebleau** the atmosphere of belle époque Paris is re-enacted with costumed actors strolling through the gardens.
**Vaux-le-Vicomte** offers candlelight tours on certain evenings. Details of all events are available at the tourist office near Marne-la-Vallée station.

# Getting There

## BY RAIL

Eurostar operates a once-daily direct service between London, Ashford International and Marne-la-Vallée station, just under a 3-minute walk from the Disney® Parks. Journey time takes just under 3 hours, making it the most convenient way to reach Disneyland® Resort Paris from anywhere in southeast England.

For information and reservations (☎ 08705 186 186; www.eurostar.com in UK). Additional Eurostar services go to Brussels and Paris via Lille, from where you can catch a direct TGV connection to Marne-la-Vallée without having to change in Paris.

## BY AIR

Paris has two main airports, Roissy-Charles de Gaulle (☎ 01 48 62 22 80), where most international flights arrive, and Orly (☎ 01 49 75 15 15). Both are served by shuttle buses *(navettes)* which depart for Disneyland Resort Paris every 20 minutes at peak times, every hour at other times. Journey times vary according to traffic density. Buses cost the same from either airport (adult €16, child €13; transfer fares are included in Disney® Hotel packages). Passengers are taken to each of the Disney Hotels (excluding Disney's Davy Crockett Ranch®) in turn, or dropped at the bus station, very near the entrance to the Disney Parks.

## BY CAR

Disneyland Resort Paris lies about 32km (20 miles) due east of Paris at Marne-la-Vallée, a diffusely defined area in the Île de France, *departement* of Seine-et-Marne. Take the A4 motorway (Autoroute de l'Est, signed Metz/Nancy), which leads to Germany, Austria and Luxembourg via Strasbourg. Disneyland Resort Paris is signed at Exit 14 (take Exit 13 for Disney's Davy Crockett Ranch).

If you approach from another direction, to avoid the capital, you will probably use the Francilienne (A104 and N104), linking motorways A1 (Autoroute du Nord, bound for the Channel ports, UK and Low Countries), A4, A6 (Autoroute du Soleil, heading south for the Riviera, Italy and Switzerland), and A10 (L'Aquitaine, which goes via Bordeaux towards Spain and Portugal). Follow signs to Marne-la-Vallée (Val d'Europe) until you see signposts for the Resort.

French motorways are free of charge in the Paris area.

Parking charges (currently €8 per day for cars; €13 for campervans; €15 for motorbikes) are waived for Disney Hotel guests, who may either park in the appropriate hotel car park, or in the main lot, which holds more than 11,000 vehicles. Note carefully where you leave your car. Each sector is named after a

Disney character. Moving walkways speed up the journey from the car park to the main entrances. Cars cannot be left overnight in the car park. If you have engine trouble ask a Cast Member for help.

## DRIVING
### Driving is on the right.
Speed limits on toll motorways (*autoroutes*) **130kph/80mph** (**110kph/70mph** when wet). Non-toll motorways and dual carriageways: **110kph/70mph** (**100kph/63mph** when wet). Paris ring road (*périphérique*): **80kph (50mph)**. Speed limits on country roads: **90kph/56mph**

(**80kph/50mph** when wet) Speed limits on urban roads: **50kph (30mph)**.

**Seat belts** must be worn in front seats at all times and in rear seats where fitted.

Random breath-testing takes place. Never drive under the influence of alcohol.

Leaded petrol is sold as *essence super* (98 octane). Unleaded is available in two grades: *essence sans plomb* (95 octane) and *essence super sans plomb* (98 octane). Diesel *(gasoil or gazole)* is also readily available. In Paris filling stations can be hard to spot.

If your car breaks down in France ☎ 17 for assistance (Police). On motorways *(autoroutes)* use the orange-coloured emergency phones (located every 2km/1 mile) to contact the breakdown service.

Various 24-hour roadside breakdown hotlines are available in France, including the one recommended and co-ordinated by the AA's 5-star insurance policy (you can only use this if you've paid up for it, of course). You may be allocated an alternative rescue service if you rent a car.

# Getting Around

## INTERNAL FLIGHTS

Air France operates the majority of domestic flights in France. Daily departures from Orly and Roissy-Charles de Gaulle airports connect Paris with most major French cities and towns in an average flight time of one hour.
Information (☎ 08 20 82 08 20).

## RER

The Parisian suburban railway (RER, pronounced 'ehr-oo-ehr') links Disneyland® Resort Paris with the city centre. There are five lines (*lignes*): A, B, C, D and E, and there are connections with the métro and SNCF suburban network.

One branch of Line A4 terminates at Marne-la-Vallée–Chessy (often known as MLV for short), which is just a couple of minutes' walk from the entrances of both Disney® Parks. It takes about about 40 minutes to get into central Paris (Châtelet–les

Halles makes a useful link to the métro). On your return journey, check the destination board carefully as it's a branched line and not all trains carry on as far as the terminus. Make sure you catch a Marne-La-Vallée train rather than one to Boissy–St-Léger). Single adult fares are €6.20 (children aged 4–11 travel for half price; under 4 free). Trains run from about 5.15am until 12.30am roughly every 10–15 minutes. Consider buying a Paris Visite ticket, valid for 1, 2, 3 or 5 days, if you plan any sightseeing.

## MÉTRO

Paris's underground with over 350 stations ensures you are never more than 500m (550yds) from a métro stop. Lines are numbered 1 to 15 and are known by the names of the stations at each end. Follow the orange *correspondance* signs to change lines. The métro runs daily 5.30am to 12.30am.

## BUSES

Buses are a good way of seeing Paris (especially route 24). Bus stops show the numbers of buses that stop there. Buses run 5.30am to 8.30pm with a reduced service on Sunday evenings. Noctambus

routes depart every hour in the week and every half-hour at weekends throughout the night. Bus tickets are the same as those for the métro.

## TAXIS

Taxis can be hailed if the roof light is on. Taxis are metered with a surcharge for luggage, journeys after 10pm and before 6.30am, and for going from and to stations and airports. Queues can be long, particularly at railway stations.

## CAR RENTAL

As an official Disney 'partner', Hertz is the most competitive rental agent for Disney package travellers. It's worth booking a deal in advance through your travel agent or Disney's Central Reservations office if you know you'll want a car. But if you are staying outside the resort, check other rental firms too (both Hertz and Avis have desks at MLV station, and many others are based at the airports). It's doubtful you'll find a rental car necessary unless you're taking a touring holiday as well as your Disneyland Resort Paris visit, or staying at Disney's Davy Crockett Ranch®, where there's no transport.

## ENTRANCE TICKETS

These are sold as 1-Day, 1-Park tickets (allowing entrance to just one park of your choice), or 1-, 2- and 3-Day Park Hopper tickets, allowing unlimited access to either Disney Park for the relevant duration. Hang on to your ticket if you want to leave the Park and return later. You don't have to use the tickets on consecutive days but check for the period of validity. Annual Passport tickets are sold in three price-bands for 300, 335 or 365 days.

Ticket prices fluctuate and quieter periods are cheaper. There isn't much difference between buying tickets in advance and buying them at the gates, but prices from UK agents vary slightly. Dozens of operators offer inclusive packages to Disneyland Resort Paris as well as Disney itself.

**Sample charges** (valid Jan 2006)
1-day, 1-park ticket: adult €46; child €38
1-day Hopper (both parks) €56/€38
2-day Hopper €103/€84
3-day Hopper €128/€105
4-day Hopper €149/€122
5-day Hopper €160/€131
Annual Passport €89–€179 (same price for child or adult; note that peak holiday periods may be excluded).

# Being There

## LOCAL TOURIST OFFICES
### DISNEYLAND® RESORT PARIS

The Île-de-France/Seine-et-Marne tourist office (small kiosk) is outside Marne-la-Vallée station and the entrance to Disney® Village.

**Espace du Tourisme d'Île-de-France et de Seine-et-Marne**
Place des Passagers-du-Vent, Disney Village, 77705, Marne-la-Vallée
☎ 01 60 43 33 33; **www.**pidf.com

### PARIS
**Office de Tourisme et des Congrès de Paris**
25 rue des Pyramides, 75001 Paris
☎ 08 92 68 30 10
**www.**paris-touristoffice.com

**Espace du Tourisme d'Île-de-France**
Carrousel du Louvre
Place de la Pyramide Inversée
99 rue de Rivoli, 75001 Paris

## EMBASSIES AND CONSULATES IN PARIS
**UK** ☎ 01 44 51 31 00
**Germany** ☎ 01 53 83 45 00
**USA** ☎ 01 43 12 22 22
**Netherlands** ☎ 01 40 62 33 00
**Spain** ☎ 01 44 43 18 00

## TELEPHONES

Both coin-operated and card phones are available in the Disney® Parks, in Disney® Village and in Resort accommodation. France Télécom phone cards are on sale at the post office, in shops and at the golf course.
Telephone charges are the same in all hotels and in the campsite. They include a mark-up over normal France Télécom rates, depending upon what time of day you call.

## INTERNATIONAL DIALLING CODES
From France to:

**UK:** 00 44
**Germany:** 00 49
**USA:** 00 1
**Spain:** 00 34

## EMERGENCY TELEPHONE NUMBERS
**Police** 17
**Fire** 18
**Ambulance (SAMU)** 15
**SOS Doctor/SOS Dentist**
01 43 37 51 00

## OPENING HOURS

Disneyland® Resort Paris can be visited 365 days a year. Usually, the Disney Parks open at 10 but often they open earlier. During peak seasons, you can usually get inside at least half an hour before the official opening time, though attractions open at the usual time. Weekdays are generally less busy than weekends, and Tuesday is especially quiet. On Monday many shops and other businesses are closed. Schools close on Wednesday, so this is a popular day for French families to visit. Closing times may vary. Although the turnstiles may allow no more visitors if the Disney Parks become too crowded; guests staying in Disney® Hotels always have entry. Check what time the Parks close as you enter: in high summer Disneyland® Park often stays open until 11pm. For details ☎ 08705 03 03 03 (from UK).

## POSTAL SERVICES

Can be found at Marne-la-Vallée–Chessy Station, usually open 9–7 daily, but not on public holidays. Stamps are sold at many shops, including The Storybook Store in Town Square, inside Disneyland Park. There are postboxes throughout the Disney Parks and Disney Hotels and Disney's Davy Crockett Ranch®.

## TIPS AND GRATUITIES

It is not necessary to leave tips in Disneyland Resort Paris, however you choose to leave something in a table-service restaurant, or to tip a Cast Member who has been especially helpful. Outside the Disney Parks check whether service is included *(service compris)* before you pay the bill. It is customary to leave small change in a saucer at a bar or café. Porters, usherettes, tour guides and cabbies all expect tips.

## HEALTH AND SAFETY

**Medical centres** First-aid centres with fully trained nursing staff are located next to Plaza Gardens Restaurant in Main Street, U.S.A.®, in Disney Village and behind Studio Services in Front Lot. Simple medical supplies can be found in all the hotels. If there is a serious problem, ask your hotel receptionist or the tourist office for advice. There is a pharmacy at Val de l'Europe, a medical centre in Esbly and a hospital in Lagny.

**Sun advice** July and August are the sunniest (and hottest) months. If you're out of doors take the usual precautions.

**Drugs** Pharmacies – recognized by their green cross sign – employ highly qualified staff able to offer medical advice, provide first-aid and prescribe a wide range of drugs, though some are available by prescription *(ordonnance)* only.

**Personal safety** Petty crime, particularly theft of wallets and handbags is fairly common in Paris. Groups of scruffy-looking children sometimes work the streets in gangs, fleecing unwary tourists. Report any loss or theft to the *Police Municipale* (blue uniforms).

## ELECTRICITY

The power supply in France is 220 volts. Sockets accept two-round-pin (or increasingly three-round-pin) plugs, so an adaptor is needed for non-Continental appliances and a voltage transformer for appliances operating on 100–120 volts.

## CURRENCY/EXCHANGE

**Currency** The unit of currency is the euro (€). Coins are in denominations of 1, 2, 5, 10, 20 and 50 cents and 1, and 2 euros. There are 100 cents in 1 euro.

Notes come in denominations of 5, 10, 20, 50, 100, 200 and 500 euros.

**Exchange** Facilities are at the Main Entrances of the Disney® Parks, and in the two information booths in Adventureland and Fantasyland. You can also change money in Disney® Village, and at any accommodation reception desk (if you are a resident). Rates are on the low side and no commission is charged. You may get a slightly better commission-free rate in central Paris. Remember that you will need your passport if you want to change traveller's cheques.

## GUIDED TOURS

Guided tours can be booked from City Hall, Town Square (Disneyland® Park) and Studio Services, Front Lot (Walt Disney Studios®). They last for 1 to 2 hours. Tours can be organized for groups by arrangement. An additional charge is made.

## CONCESSIONS

**Senior citizens** Groups of 25 senior citizens (over 55s) or more qualify for a 20 per cent reduction (not always valid during peak periods). Cast members are always happy to help anyone with special needs. Carte Senior, valid for all women over 60 and all men over 65, entitles the bearer to reductions of up to 50 per cent in Paris museums, on public transport and in places of entertainment. The card costs about €50 for unlimited travel. To get one, take your passport to the Abonnement (ticket) office of any main railway station. The card is valid for a year. If you do not have one, wave your passport when paying and you may still be able to get a discount.

## VISITORS WITH DISABILITIES
Ask for the *Disabled Guest Guide* at the main entrance of Disneyland® Park, City Hall or at Studio Services. The Resort is designed to be user-friendly, but wheelchair users will need to find someone who can lift them out of their chair and on to rides (Cast Members are not allowed to do this). Special vehicles can be provided to help guests reach the Disney Parks from the hotels, and all hotels have rooms designed for those with disabilities. Parking spaces near the entrance are also available. Wheelchairs can be rented in Town Square in Main Street, U.S.A.® or at Studio Services in Front Lot (€7.50 per day, deposit €150; they must not be taken outside the Disney Parks). All WC blocks, shops and restaurants are accessible by wheelchair, and some shops have special dressing-rooms. If you need assistance,

enquire at City Hall, First Aid (near Plaza Gardens Restaurant) or Studio Services. If you have a weak back or neck, avoid the joltier rides. Special aids are available for guests with sight impairments.

## CHARGES
These prices were current at the time of going to press but check before visiting. Children over 12 count as adults and pay full price. Children under three can enter free.

**1-day Disney Park Entrance Ticket:** (high or low-season): adult €42, child (3–11) €34
**2-day 'Hopper' Ticket:** adult €93, child €77
**3-day 'Hopper' Ticket:** adult €113, child €92
**2-Park Annual Ticket:** adult €229, child €199
**Car parking:** €8 per day
**VEA Airport Shuttle:** €16 (single adult), €13 (child)
**RER to/from central Paris:** €6.20 (single adult), €3.10 (child)
**Animal Care Center:** €8 per day (including food), or €12 overnight
**Wheelchair or pushchair rental:** €7.50 per day; deposit €150 (not to be taken outside the Disney Parks)
**Buffalo Bill's Wild West Show (Disney Village):** adult €59, child €39 (drinks and dinner included).

# The story so far

© Disney

# The shaping of Disneyland® Resort Paris

The idea of a Disney® Park in Europe goes back over 30 years, though it was not until 1984 that The Walt Disney Company began to explore the possibilities seriously. The options were wide open. Would English-speaking Britain, whose citizens so eagerly patronize American Theme Parks, naturally play host to Mickey Mouse? Or should the new Disney Park be blessed with that cocktail of sunshine and oranges so successful in California and Florida – by being located in southern Spain, perhaps? Why not target the wealthy Germans? No doubt they could run the show as efficiently as Walt would have wished. Feasibility studies spawned; Team Disney anguished, and then began some hard bargaining.

Eventually, the keys to the kingdom fell into French hands. The promised land was a stretch of unprepossessing sugar-beet fields about 32km (20 miles) east of Paris. Not immediately enticing, but the Marne-la-Vallée area had a number of advantages. For one thing, it was available. And there are not that many suitably sized tracts of affordable land available in Western Europe these days. Secondly, it lay slap in the middle of a cat's cradle of important communication networks linking the richest and most densely populated countries of Europe. And thirdly, it was on the eastern outskirts of the greater Paris area. It was, admittedly, a bit damper and chillier than one might have hoped, but you can't have everything.

## ONCE UPON A TIME

The Walt Disney Company signed a 30-year contract to develop the site with the French authorities in 1987. The French government purchased some 1,940ha (4,800 acres) of land, a total area about one-fifth the size of Paris, agreeing to release it to Disney as it was needed. Meanwhile, residents and farmers, now tenants instead of landlords, carried on their lives as normally as they could in a region destined for rapid and irrevocable change. Earth-moving and construction equipment arrived to shift millions of tons of topsoil into new configurations of lakes, railway tracks, road systems and protective circular ramparts, like some Iron Age hill fort.

The statistics were awesome, and the speed at which the project took shape was astonishing. Within four years Phase I of the development was complete, covering 600ha (1,483 acres) of land. The region was transformed, with 450,000 trees and shrubs, artificial expanses of water, and almost 32km (20 miles) of roads. Six extraordinary hotels and a 'trapper village' emerged from the fields, but more curious structures could be glimpsed behind the stockade surrounding the new Disney Park – a storybook castle, a piece of re-created Arizona and a skull-like cave.

## AGAINST THE ODDS

Meanwhile, around the edges of the complex, speculation buzzed, both of the cerebral and mercenary kinds. Rumours of Disney's sinister transatlantic masterplan to undermine 'French Culture As We Know It Today' were fuelled, and many a pundit had a scornful crack at Mickey Mouse.

Not everyone liked the idea of a Disney Park on their doorstep. And, of course, some of the locals had to play the role of dispossessed serfs carefully, to maximize any potential return on their lost land. A crocodile tear or two would not be inappropriate in the circumstances. This controversial climate did not stop entrepreneurs from constructing motels and petrol stations in many of the surrounding villages. These extraneous developments, simply cashing in on the Disney bandwagon, have done most to disrupt the area. Sadly, they are an inevitable consequence of such a huge investment, readily predictable from all the experiences of American Theme Parks.

Other unintentional effects of Disney's impact on this part of France are less tangible, but still worrying. A glance at local tourist literature produces the disconcerting sensation that the whole of the Seine-et-Marne region is turning into a sort of giant Theme Park. Many local authorities, spurred to enterprise by Disney's example, are now promoting their tourist portfolios strongly as rival (or rather, supplementary) attractions. Every little sight and mildly pretty village is now paraded before the eyes of Disney patrons like some contestant in a game show. Summer pageants, medieval banquets and candlelit tours abound. With all this going on, there is a strong possibility that some visitors at least, dazed by the razzmatazz, will come to regard the great châteaux of the Île-de-France as mere clones of the Sleeping Beauty Castle.

## HAPPY EVER AFTER

For those who recognize the difference, however, the historic and cultural riches of the surroundings (including Paris, of course) must be regarded as one of the most appealing features of Disneyland® Resort Paris. In the US, at Orlando and Anaheim, there are dozens of things to do, but they are an oddly monochromatic mix of Theme Parks and contrived re-creation. In France the texture of the holiday tapestry is infinitely more interesting and complex.

Controversy has now died down as the positive influence of the Disney® Parks on the area's economy is hard to deny. The creation of over 10,000 jobs at the resort and an estimated 30,000 in the

Île-de-France region, as well as spin-offs for hoteliers and other local businesses, has been most welcome. The infrastructure of the area (road and rail connections, hotel accommodation, and so on) has been boosted out of all recognition. The region was now ready to welcome the Walt Disney Studios® Park, which opened its gates in March 2002, a few days before the 10th anniversary of Disneyland® Resort Paris.

The idea of a second European Disney® Park on the theme of cinema, animation and television goes back to 1992, just before Disneyland® Park opened, but Disney® Imagineers were only given the green light to begin planning and designing the new Disney Park in 1997. They based their work on the concept of the successful Disney-MGM Studios at Walt Disney World® in Florida and adapted their new creation to European audiences with the help of European professionals in the world of cinema, such as Rémy Julienne, the French stunt designer.

Some agonize, justifiably enough, over the un-Frenchness of it all. There are nods and winks at European fairy stories and children's classics, but basically Disneyland Resort Paris is a heartily transatlantic product, as American as a prime rib steak. French culture, however, is nothing if not robust. The things many people love about France and the French way of life will survive the arrival of Mickey Mouse perfectly well. In any case, before we complain too loudly about the invasion of an alien culture, maybe there are some things about the land of Mickey Mouse that we Europeans should take note of: what, after all, is wrong with clean toilets, courteous staff, efficient transport systems and litter-free grounds?

For the Resort to be a success, all Disney needed was for enough people to turn up and enjoy themselves, and then tell their friends. This goal was easily reached, for enjoying yourself at Disneyland Resort Paris is almost unavoidable. Where else can grown-up people ride on an elephant roundabout, or wear mouse ears, without feeling like idiots?

# Walt Disney

Walter Elias Disney was born in Chicago, Illinois, in 1901, the fourth of five children in a family of slender means. His father was a struggling building contractor whose varied enterprises consistently failed. When they did, the family doggedly moved on, first to Marceline, then to Kansas City, Missouri. Walt's unsettled upbringing gave him only a rudimentary education, and he spent his spare time living on his wits, delivering newspapers door-to-door and hawking sodas on trains. During a brief stint of ambulance-driving in France at the end of World War I (he was too young to join up), he first exercised his artistic talents commercially, painting camouflage helmets and adding fake bullet holes. After the war Walt returned to Kansas City and found a job drawing for an advertising agency. There he met a talented Dutch artist, Ub Iwerks, and together they set up a company, Laugh-o-Gram Films. It soon went to the wall but, like all true romantics of his day, Walt was hopelessly hooked on the glamour of celluloid. With a small fistful of dollars, he set off to try his luck in Hollywood, followed by Ub. From then on Walt had little contact with his parents. But he always kept up with his elder brother Roy, with whom he later set up in business to produce short cartoons. In 1925 Walt married Lillian Bounds, who lived with his erratic genius for over 40 years.

After many false starts and financial failures (one of which involved the loss of his prize cartoon character, Oswald the Lucky Rabbit, to an unprincipled distributor), Walt's big break came in 1928, using a new character called Mickey Mouse. The film was *Steamboat Willie*, the first animated film to use synchronized sound. Mickey's squeaks and sighs were Walt Disney's own. Roy Disney attempted to temper Walt's wilder impulses with sensible financial caution, but Walt, always cavalier about the money side, was an incorrigible enthusiast, an ideas man, a risk-taker. And his instincts were sound. He could spot a good story at a thousand paces (and shamelessly borrow it, if necessary) and then would edit it brilliantly for his own medium. Above all else, he was a

© Disney

maniacal perfectionist. Every last detail had to be right. All his life he worked obsessively hard, even coming dangerously close to a nervous breakdown in 1931.

Slowly the Disney studios began to prosper with full-length animations like *Snow White and the Seven Dwarfs*, *Pinocchio* and *Fantasia*. After World War II the Disney brothers seized the opportunities offered by the new era of television. Their Disneyland® programme (set up, in part, to fund the first Disney® Park) was a great success. From animated films, Disney moved on to using live actors in comedies, wildlife pictures and adventure stories like *Treasure Island*. The core of the business was always safe, clean, family entertainment for the post-war era. The films sold like hot cakes.

Walt first dreamed of theme parks in the 1930s, and the Magic Kingdom® in California finally opened in 1953. In 1966 his permanent smoker's cough developed a more sinister note, and by December, just a week after his 65th birthday, he was dead – before he could witness the opening of his Florida park.

Few film producers have captured the imagination, influenced so many people, and aroused such loyalty, loathing and passionate interest as Walt Disney. Forty years after his death, debate still rages over the influence of his work – even more over the colossal empire he created to perpetuate it. Through this he has achieved a strangely alarming immortality. So, too, has his single most memorable creation: Mickey Mouse, now nearly 80 years old.

# Background

In the 1930s Walt began imagining how he could improve on the dreary theme parks he took his daughters to see, but it was only after the war that his obsession developed to fever pitch. At that time amusement parks were bracketed with funfairs and circuses as tawdry and disreputable places. Walt found it very difficult to convey his vision of a place of fun and fantasy in an orderly, civilized setting. He wanted to create a place where both adults and children could enjoy themselves together and come away feeling better. He wanted themes that reflected his Utopian faith in technological progress and the future, a haven in which the archetypal American virtues of pluck and innocence could flourish.

In 1955 Disneyland® Park (also known as 'the Magic Kingdom®'), the world's first Theme Park, opened at Anaheim, in Orange County, California. Roy refused to let Walt have the money to build it; he had to cash in his life insurance. But the enterprise succeeded, and the world flocked to see it. Walt began to dream of other Theme Parks, his ambitions growing like beanstalks for a brave new world – a model of planning and innovative lifestyles.

A second site was chosen: the ill-drained acres of central Florida, another 'Orange County'. Quietly the land was purchased on Disney's behalf at knock-down prices through various agencies. Sadly, Walt Disney never lived to see his Floridian dream realized. It was left to his heirs to construct Walt Disney World® Resort from the blueprint. This second Disney® Park complex opened in Orlando in 1971, much larger and more ambitious than anything in California.

Twelve years later, in 1983, another Disneyland Park appeared in Tokyo. Soon afterwards, talented chief executive Michael Eisner, recruited from Paramount, was setting a firm course for the floundering Disney empire, which for several years after its founder's death had seemed to lose its way. Throughout the 1980s the Theme Parks boomed, and revenues from television and merchandising soared. By the middle of the decade plans for a European park were firmly on the drawing board.

Disneyland® Resort Paris has undergone a white-knuckle financial roller-coaster since its inauguration, but the mood was confident enough in 2005 for yet another Disneyland to open, this time in Hong Kong. Disney's acquisition of Pixar Animation Studios and the recruitment of its chief executive Steve Jobs (who is also head of Apple Computer) can only strengthen its stake in the worlds of entertainment and communications technology.

## IMAGINEERS®

Any operation on the scale of a Disney® Park requires colossal planning and co-operative effort, but just how much goes on behind the scenes may surprise you. A whole workforce of Disney employees called 'Imagineers' devotes its time and energy to inventing and realizing the attractions. These artists and technicians are the ones who make illusion reality, working with models and micro-cameras, experimenting with innumerable materials, designs and ideas, studying every last detail for authenticity. It is a serious business: careers have been made and broken over the height of some of the buildings. The complexity of all this is fascinating, though most of the illusions are hidden or barely perceived by the vast majority of visitors.

When you enter Disneyland® Park, notice how far away the castle seems as you look down Main Street, U.S.A.® Why do some of the other buildings seem so accessible? It is all done with clever angles and techniques called 'forced perspective'. Upper storeys are often rather smaller than their proper size, with every architectural detail carefully scaled down. These illusions are just 3-D versions of the kinds of things Disney constantly practised in his films. What the eye sees is not necessarily what is really there, as any animation specialist knows.

## AUDIO–ANIMATRONICS®

This Disney-patented system of animating figures (animals, plants, birds and robots as well as humans) has now reached levels of great technical sophistication, and some amazingly lifelike effects can be created. Striking examples of this new technology are the rowdy pirates in the Pirates of the Caribbean attraction in Adventureland. Best of all, without a doubt, is the wonderful dragon that lurks beneath the Sleeping Beauty Castle.

## CAST MEMBERS

Anywhere else, these people would be called Theme Park staff. But here they are the cast – everyone from that fellow sweeping up spilt popcorn to Sleeping Beauty herself.

How do they rehearse for that relentless PR exercise, constantly smiling and helpful? They go to university! The Disney University, where appropriate cheerful responses are drilled into prospective Cast Members, and deviant tendencies like tattoos, red nail polish and facial hair are rigorously drilled out. However, some concessions have been made to French fashion: red lipstick may be worn, tastefully. And who are you? You are the guests at this show.

## DISNEY CHARACTERS

Minnie and Mickey and the other Disney Character favourites are a popular and ubiquitous feature of the Disney® Parks. They communicate in their own special way putting the guests at ease, although younger children may sometimes be overwhelmed to meet some of their favourite Disney friends. If you want an autograph, make sure you open the book at a suitable page, and have a pen ready to hand.

# Dos and Don'ts

**Some dos...**
- Remember to bring a sweater, light rainwear and to wear comfortable shoes.
- Shoes and shirts must be worn at all times.
- Reduce waiting time by making use of the FASTPASS® service (► opposite).
- Children under seven must be accompanied by an adult.
- Make sure you have your entrance ticket with you if you leave either Disney® Park so that you can get back in again.
- Check on closing times.
- Pick up an Entertainment Programme from City Hall in Disneyland® Park or Studio Services in Walt Disney Studios® Park.
- Life is easier if you use a credit card. Visa, MasterCard or American Express are widely accepted. Guests staying at a Disneyland® Resort Paris hotel will be given a chargecard that can be used within the Resort.
- Visit the tourist office next to the RER station if you are thinking about touring outside the Resort (☎ 01 60 43 33 33, daily 9am–8.45pm).

**...and some don'ts**
- Smoking, eating and drinking are not allowed inside attractions and in queuing areas. Hotel table service restaurants are all non-smoking. All table-service restaurants in the Disney Parks are designated non-smoking. A picnic area located between Guest Parking and the Disney Parks Entrance is intended for guests bringing their own food.
- No pets, except guide dogs, are allowed to enter the Parks. They may be left at the Animal Care Centre near the car park on production of a certificate of health, or verification of vaccination. A service charge applies (► 21).
- Do not leave personal belongings unattended.
- No flash photography or video taping are allowed inside the attractions.

© Disney

**FASTPASS®**
This free time-saving service is designed to cut waiting times at the following popular attractions at the Disneyland Park.

● Indiana Jones™ and the Temple of Peril, Space Mountain: Mission 2, Big Thunder Mountain, Peter Pan's Flight, Star Tours, Buzz Lightyear Laser Blast.

● If you insert your Park entrance ticket into the machine at the entrance to your chosen attraction, you will receive another ticket for a one-hour time slot later in the day.

● Return during this period, and you can join a priority queue, thus reducing your waiting time.

● Once the time slot for your ticket starts, you can get a FASTPASS for another attraction.

● Obviously there's no point in everyone having a FASTPASS ticket, so numbers are limited, and may run out by lunchtime.

● It makes sense to visit popular attractions as early as possible.

# Features of
# Disneyland® Resort Paris

**It is well worth spending some time familiarizing yourself with the layout of Disneyland® Resort Paris and the Disney® Parks, particularly if you only have one or two days to see everything. Those hours spent in the Disney Parks will be expensive if you waste time, but if you use them well you will not be disappointed. Study the maps of the Parks, which although not to scale, both show Disney® Village, the parking area and hotels in relation to the Disney Parks.**

## DISNEYLAND RESORT PARIS

Disneyland Resort Paris covers a total land area measuring one-fifth the size of Paris. When you hear that there is still room for development, you realize the gigantic proportions of the project! At present the Resort includes seven themed Disney® Hotels, another half-dozen Selected/Associated hotels and apartments, a 27-hole golf course, the Disney Village entertainment centre, the Disneyland® Park, which alone represents 57ha (140 acres), and the Walt Disney Studios® Park, 25ha (62 acres) at opening stage.

Exit roads from surrounding routes lead smoothly along newly constructed dual carriageways to all parts of the Resort, with all hotels and the main car park clearly signposted from exit 14 of the A4 motorway. For Disney's Davy Crockett Ranch® take exit 13. If you need petrol, you will find it by Disney's Hotel Santa Fe®. From the large visitor's car park (remember in which section you leave your vehicle), covered moving walkways lead to a wide avenue that heads straight for the parks' entrance and ticket offices past the film-set décor of Disney Village on the left. If you have a pet, you must leave it at the Animal Care Centre next to the parking area, where a service charge applies (► Charges, 21). At the end of the moving walkways there is a picnic area. There is a car park for disabled visitors nearer the entrance. The entrance gates of the

Walt Disney Studios Park are clearly visible from the glass dome of the RER station. Spanned by the unmissable Disneyland® Hotel is the entrance to the Disneyland Park.

If you arrive by commuter train you will emerge at the Marne-la-Vallée–Chessy RER station, very close to the entrance to both Disney Parks. There is a post office inside the station. Next to it is the TGV-Eurostar station, terminal point of the express link joining several major European rail networks.

Several expanses of artificially created water form scenic vistas within the Resort area. Lake Disney® is surrounded by three hotels, each representing a typical aspect of the American scene: Disney's Hotel New York®, Disney's Sequoia Lodge® and Disney's Newport Bay Club®. Two more hotels, Disney's Hotel Santa Fe® and Disney's Hotel Cheyenne®, straddle the Rio Grande, a canal northeast of Lake Disney®. There are traffic-free promenades on either side of the water, making the route between the Disney Parks and the Resort Hotels a pleasant walk, but a free shuttle bus is available. Disney's Davy Crockett Ranch®, situated at the heart of a forested area and symbolizing the American pioneer spirit, is a 15-minute drive from the Disney Parks (no shuttle bus runs).

## DISNEY® VILLAGE

Opposite the RER station, this startling enertainment complex re-creates the atmosphere of a typical American town: angular metallic structures decorated in zigzag patterns tower above ochre-coloured saloons and bars along a brad walkway leading to the edge of Lake Disney, where a colourful hot-air balloon instantly catches the eye. PanoraMagique is the world's largest captive balloon, giving the chance to float 100m (328ft) above the resort for a spectacular six-minute bird's-eye view.

During the day the sun glitters on the shiny aluminium and mosaic panels; at night the area is a maze of balloons rocking to the sound of live concerts. This bold modern structure, designed by architect Frank Gehry, offers entertainment, eating and shopping facilities to Disneyland® Resort Paris visitors during the day and keeps them happy after the Disney® Parks have closed. It consists of shops, restaurants, bars and night spots, including a nightclub and the popular Buffalo Bill's Wild West Show. It also has a multiplex Gaumont cinema incorporating a giant IMAX screen (English films are shown occasionally), and an indoor leisure centre (NEX) with a bowling alley and arcade games.

Additional services include a Travelex *bureau de change*. Just outside the Disney® Village is the tourist office for the local Île-de-France region, and a parking lot with 1,340 places. Disney Village is open daily free of charge, except on one or two special holidays.

## DISNEY PARKS

A practical approach is necessary if you want to make the most of the Disney magic. Facilities and services at both Disney Parks are designed to ensure that you enjoy yourself to the full. Bulky articles you will not need during your visit can be handed in at Guest Storage (service charge), situated outside the Disneyland® Park entrance, close to the Guest Relations office, and just inside Walt Disney Studios® Park, next to Studios Service. Note that the self-service, coin-operated lockers just inside the entrance gates of Disneyland Park are no longer in use for security reasons.

Inside the gates, get your bearings as quickly as possible. Look at the map given to you at the turnstiles. Walt Disney Studios Park is divided into four production areas, starting with the Front Lot overlooked by the Studios Water Tower with mouse ears.

Once inside the Disney Parks, don't be dazzled by the lure of the landmark Earrfel Tower, a water tower with mouse ears, or the enchanting Sleeping Beauty Castle. Take time to look around the Mediterranean-style courtyard at Walt Disney Studios Park, Place des Frères Lumières, or the early 20th-century Town Square in Disneyland Park, both of which have useful services and facilities.

Disneyland Park is also divided, rather like a pie chart, into five separate thematic areas or Lands. Beyond Main Street, U.S.A.®.

stretching ahead of you lies the park's central landmark, Sleeping Beauty Castle, its spindly turrets thrusting into the sky.

Studio Services (Walt Disney Studios Park) and City Hall (Disneyland Park), both situated just inside the gates, are the main information centres and are well worth a visit: they are a convenient meeting place for families and friends, and messages can also be left here.

Guide maps in several languages, Park information, guide books for guests with disabilities and information in braille are available at the desks. Pick up a copy of the Insider's Guide leaflet, full of useful tips on how to make the most of your visit. You can also book a room, a restaurant, a dinner-show or a Character Tea; check the times of the shows and parades; change your money at bureaux de change; or make reservations for a guided walking tour of either or both Disney Parks (one-hour tours of Walt Disney Studios Park, two-hour tours of Disneyland Park).

If it's a pushchair (stroller) or wheelchair you need, you can rent one by the day near Studio Services in Walt Disney Studios Park or across Town Square from City Hall in Disneyland Park; a padlock is useful to keep your pushchair safe while you take young children on rides. Note that Cast Members are not available to accompany guests in wheelchairs or to look after children while their parents enjoy attractions that are unsuitable for youngsters.

However, Disneyland Resort Paris has found a way to alleviate adult frustration in this case called Baby Switch, which allows both parents to enjoy the attraction without having to stand in the queue twice (ask for more information from the Cast Members at the entrance to the attraction). The Lost and Found office is next to Studio Services at the entrance to Walt Disney Studios Park and at City Hall in Disneyland Park.

Before you leave the Town Square to explore the rest of Disneyland® Park, bear in mind that this is a good place to watch the Parade and take pictures from different angles as the floats slowly make their way round the square; a spot is reserved for people in wheelchairs in front of Ribbons & Bows Hat Shop.

Now that you have everything you need and are in the right mood, you can uncover the magic of cinema at Walt Disney Studios® Park. Or at Disneyland Park, you can walk down Main Street, U.S.A.®, hop on one of the nostalgic vehicles bound for Central Plaza or embark on a journey round Disneyland Park aboard one of the steam trains of the Disneyland® Railroad. When you get to Central Plaza, you will see the Plaza Gardens Restaurant on your right; next to it are three more services that might prove useful at some time during your visit: the First Aid Centre, the Baby Care Centre and the Lost Children Point. Equivalent facilities are also located behind Studio Services in Walt Disney Studios Park.

If you find yourself running short of funds while you are inside the Disney® Parks, there are automatic cash dispensers next to Studio Services and at Backlot Express Restaurant in Walt Disney Studios Park. In Disneyland Park they are in the arcades parallel to Main Street, U.S.A., in Adventureland and in Discoveryland.

Opening times, operating procedures and so on are subject to change without notice, and it is always advisable to check with Guest Relations for up-to-date information. Occasionally attractions may be closed for technical reasons (such as safety checks) or only open in summer (such as Autopia or Storybook Land).

## MAKE THE MOST OF YOUR VISIT

Your action plan depends very much on what sort of ticket you have. The most popular 'Entrance Passports', as Disneyland tickets are called, are 1-Day 1-Park Passports, allowing access to just one Park, or Park Hopper tickets, giving unlimited access to both Disney Parks for a specified duration. If you have booked a Disneyland package holiday, a Park Hopper entrance ticket will almost certainly be included in the deal.

If you have bought just a 1-Day, 1-Park entrance ticket, you will first have to decide which Disney Park you want to visit. If you decide to spend the day in Disneyland Park, you will have to tackle the Park like a military exercise if you want to see it all. Get there early and head for the popular rides first (Big Thunder Mountain or Space Mountain: Mission 2), making the most of slack periods (for example, during mealtimes, the parades or in the evening). You will obviously get more value out of your ticket if you choose a time when Disneyland Park stays open late (in summer, or at peak holiday times). A useful time-saver is the free FASTPASS® (➤ 39), available at several attractions in Disneyland Park.

A 2- or 3-day ticket obviously gives you more time to experience the Disney Parks. In addition, you can take a rest whenever you want to, and do the things you like best more than once. Remember, you don't have to use your ticket on consecutive days, and if you are staying at the resort for several days, it is a good idea to have a break at some point – see Excursions suggestions (➤ 104–113). Then come back and have another day at the Disney Parks. Most people can get at least two days' fun out of Disneyland® Resort Paris, and keen theme-parkers will want even longer. Not everyone likes theme parks, of course, so there's a remote chance you may just hate it once you get inside. But there's a much bigger chance that you will want to spend more time here than you have available.

If you do buy a 3-day ticket, do not try to see the whole of either Disney Park on day one. Save some of the excitement for your next visit. In Disneyland Park visit Main Street, U.S.A., the Sleeping Beauty Castle, Fantasyland and Discoveryland on day one, and then go to Frontierland and Adventureland on day two. You can try out your favourite rides again, have a relaxing lunch, look round all the shops, or even leave the Disney® Parks for a nap or a swim at your hotel on day three. It is particularly important to prevent children from becoming overtired. Particularly if the weather is hot, make sure they get enough to drink and are protected from the sun. No two children react in quite the same way to the attractions at the Disney Parks. Most take them in a matter-of-fact way, and some are completely blasé, others might be completely overwhelmed by the scale of the attractions. It is quite difficult to assess what may alarm a child. Very young ones may find the spooks in Phantom Manor, the eerier sections of Pirates of the Caribbean, or the Wicked Queen in Snow White and the Seven Dwarfs quite perturbing.

Here is a brief run-down of attractions, showing which ones may suit your party.

## YOUNG CHILDREN

Very young children will best enjoy the rides on Main Street, U.S.A®, the Sleeping Beauty Castle and Fantasyland with its fairy-tale theme rides: Peter Pan's Flight, Pinocchio's Fantastic Journey, Snow White and the Seven Dwarfs, Casey Jr – le Petit Train du Cirque or Storybook Land; you could also try your luck with Alice's Curious Labyrinth and 'it's a small world'. Take them for a gentle boat ride round the Rivers of the Far West, and visit Critter Corral to see some real live animals. Make sure they get a chance to meet Mickey Mouse at some point, too. They will probably enjoy the Swiss Family Robinson Treehouse and a ride on one of the steam trains. See the shows at Fantasy Festival Stage, Chaparral Theatre or the Royal Castle Stage. Also, catch the daytime parade, even if the Fantillusion Parade (on certain dates through the year) is past bedtime.

© Disney

## OLDER CHILDREN

After seeing the Sleeping Beauty Castle,
head for Frontierland, Adventureland and
Discoveryland. After gaining their
confidence on a few rides, many children
want to try absolutely everything, including
Dumbo the Flying Elephant and Le
Carrousel de Lancelot, which may seem
too babyish for them at first. Adventurous
types will enjoy Frontierland, Adventureland
and Discoveryland, so go to them when
you have seen the Sleeping Beauty Castle.
After a few rides they may want to try
absolutely everything, even 'baby rides' like
Dumbo the Flying Elephant and Lancelot's
Carousel, but they may scorn Fantasyland's
younger appeal at first.

## A SPOT OF ADRENALIN

Frontierland attractions include a runaway
mine train at Big Thunder Mountain and a
scary visit to Phantom Manor. Have a go at
shooting bank robbers at the Rustler
Roundup Shootin' Gallery (you will need
extra euros for this). In Adventureland try
the rope and plank bridges, and Indiana
Jones™ and the Temple of Peril. In
Discoveryland go for maximum throttle in a
'car of the future' on Autopia (the race-
track), pilot a spaceship in Orbitron®,
or take a ride through outer space in Star
Tours and Space Mountain: Mission 2.
Volunteer for Honey, I Shrunk the Audience,
an amazing shrinking experience with visual

and tactile effects. On summer evenings watch out for the exciting fireworks show called Wishes (selected dates only).

## RESTRICTIONS
No children under three are allowed to ride on Star Tours; none under one on Orbitron, Peter Pan's Flight, Casey Jr – le Petit Train du Cirque and Armageddon Special Effects. There are minimum height restrictions on Big Thunder Mountain, Crush's Coaster, Dumbo the Flying Elephant, Indiana Jones™ and the Temple of Peril, Space Mountain: Mission 2 and Autopia in Disneyland® Park and on Rock 'n' Roller Coaster starring Aerosmith and Cyberspace Mountain in Walt Disney Studios® Park. If you suffer from motion sickness you may be wise to avoid Big Thunder Mountain, Space Mountain: Mission 2, Orbitron®, the Mad Hatter's Tea Cups and Rock 'n' Roller Coaster starring Aerosmith, though an excess of ice-cream is usually more to blame for any queasiness. Honey, I Shrunk the Audience and Moteurs…Action! Stunt Show Spectacular® is fairly loud and intense. If you are pregnant, or have high blood pressure, a weak back, heart or neck, avoid jolting rides.

## CHILD FACILITIES
Child facilities are well publicized throughout the Parks. There is a Baby Care Centre in Main Street, U.S.A.® (Disneyland Park) or behind Studio Services (Walt Disney Studios® Park) where nappies (diapers) can be changed, bottles warmed and basic necessities purchased. Pushchairs (strollers) can be rented for use within the Parks in Town Square (Disneyland Park) or near Studio Services (Walt Disney Studios Park). There are no restrictions on pushchairs being brought into the Disney® Parks. Lost children will be taken to the Lost Children Point and looked after until you find them. Child menus or child-sized portions and high chairs are available in most restaurants, and cots on request in all Disney® Hotels (free of charge).

And if after enjoying a day with the family in the Parks, parents want to have a night out on their own, all the Disney Hotels provide babysitting services.

# Exploring

© Disney

© Disney

# Disneyland® Park

**Disneyland® Park transmits on a grand scale the Disney magic that has enchanted several generations of children and the young at heart. Here mesmerizing characters welcome visitors to a land where dreams come true, where make-believe is real, where imagination becomes reality. Feel the excitement and laughter as you stroll down Main Street, U.S.A.®, gateway to other themed Lands in the Disneyland Park, Frontierland, Adventureland, Fantasyland and Discoveryland. Through shows, parades and thrilling attractions for all ages relive the legendary era of the Wild West, encompass an adventure through the Middle East, African jungles and tropical islands, see your favourite fairy-tales come to life and discover the futuristic sensation waiting at every turn.**

© Disney

# Main Street, U.S.A.®

©DISNEY

The scene is set by the flamboyant Victorian splendour of the Disneyland® Hotel spanning the entrance gates, even before you pass through the turnstiles into Station Plaza. Once visitors emerge into Town Square from Main Street Station, they are in small-town America at about the turn of the 20th century (as those of us who never saw it like to imagine it might have been). It is a world of gas lamps and horse-drawn streetcars, decorative lettering and absurdly pretty architecture, all in the colours of Italian ice-cream. Each minutely detailed façade in Town Square and Main Street, U.S.A.® is different, but the ornate balustrades and bargeboards, pediments and parapets seem to be in perfect scale and harmony. This is a magnificent piece of deception by the Disney Imagineers® – the top storeys are subtly graduated in size, so that the Sleeping Beauty Castle appears much farther away than it really is. All the street furniture – lamp-posts, letter-boxes, litter-bins, fire hydrants – have been carefully designed to suit the period.

© Disney

Main Street, U.S.A. is the orientation centre of the Park, where you can ask for information, store belongings, rent wheelchairs

© Disney

or pushchairs (strollers), book guided tours, find out about lost property (or people), and generally warm to the Disneyland® Park mood as marching bands keep up a brisk tempo. The rest of Main Street, U.S.A. is devoted mostly to shops and eating places. In Town Square there are neat municipal gardens, park benches and a gazebo, where you can board one of the period vehicles to transport you down Main Street, U.S.A., which links Town Square with the hub of the Park, Central Plaza, beside which the Sleeping Beauty Castle stands. From here you can choose which of the lands to see next. If you prefer, you can take a train from Main Street Station, located up steps just inside Town Square, and either go on a complete circuit of the Disneyland Park to get your bearings, or get off at Frontierland, Fantasyland or Discoveryland.

© Disney

## ARCADES

There are two covered passageways on either side of Main Street, U.S.A.® with rear access to the restaurants and shops. Inside they are beautifully decorated in fin-de-siècle style, with wrought-iron work and pretty gas lamps. Liberty Arcade, on the left side of Main Street, U.S.A. as you face the castle, contains an exhibition about the Statue of Liberty, with plans, drawings, photographs and the Statue of Liberty Tableau. This is a diorama about the unveiling of the monument – a diplomatic touch by Disney, emphasizing Franco-American friendship and collaboration. The inaugural ceremony took place in New York harbour in 1886. The 33m (108ft) statue by the French sculptor Frédéric-Auguste Bartholdi is made of bronze strips fixed to a steel frame designed by Gustave Eiffel, who made the headlines barely three years later when his famous tower was inaugurated for the 1889 World Exhibition. Liberty was a gift from the French people to the American people to celebrate the centenary of the American War of Independence and French involvement in it. Discovery Arcade, on the right side of Main Street, U.S.A., features cabinets displaying various inventions from the early 20th-century flying machines to strange sporting equipment. Fun to look at if you have lots of spare time.

## DISNEYLAND RAILROAD

These charming steam engines chug around the perimeter of Disneyland® Park, stopping at Main Street, U.S.A., Frontierland Depot, and Fantasyland and Discoveryland stations. No Disney Resort would be complete without an old train or two, for nostalgic railways were one of Walt's abiding passions. He even had a complete track with scaled-down engine and carriages built in his garden. At Disneyland Park there are four individual, authentically styled locomotives, all beautifully painted and fitted and evoking the great railroad days of late-19th-century America. One is a Presidential Train of the type used by government officials, another a pioneering Wild West Train, the third an East Coast Excursion Train. The fourth is called *Eureka* as a reminder of the famous cry which echoed throughout America in 1849 and started the Gold Rush. The engines were manufactured by Welsh boilermakers with every detail carefully in place: whistles, smoke-stacks, cowcatchers and shiny brass fittings. These engines genuinely run on steam produced by water going through a diesel boiler, a departure from authenticity deliberately made by the pollution-conscious Disney team. Each engine fills up with water from the Frontierland tank every hour or so. The carriages are open on one side, giving good views of the Disneyland Park. Each train can take about 270 passengers, and one arrives about every 10 minutes; it takes 20 minutes to go right round Disneyland Park. On the journey between Main Street Station and Frontierland Depot the train passes through Grand Canyon Diorama (➤ 66).

© Disney

## DISNEY PARADES

Disney theme parks are famous for their parades, which are a major attraction and focal point of Main Street, U.S.A.® They are elaborate, colourful spectacles like carnival processions, with lots of floats, lights and music. They generally start near Fantasyland and proceed down Main Street, U.S.A.

You will find the area very crowded. Stake out a good vantage point in advance. An expensive way to do it is to visit Walt's – an American Restaurant. If you are lucky enough to get a window table, you should get a good view of the parades from the upper floor. Views from the other Main Street, U.S.A. restaurants are distant, or will probably be blocked by kerb-side spectators, but you may be lucky in Plaza Gardens.

Traditional daytime parades includes 'Disney's Once Upon a Dream' Parade, which features famous dream moments from the best-loved Disney stories. Seasonally themed parades take place during holiday periods, particularly at Christmas. Disney The new Disney Characters' Express gives guests opportunities to meet favourite Disney Characters as they travel down Main Steet several times a day. On summer evenings when the Disneyland® Park remains open until later, Disney's® Fantillusion© parade is definitely worth catching for its spectacular

floats illuminated by thousands of twinkling lights. Magnificent firework shows sometimes bring the evening's entertainment to a climax. All shows and parades take place on selected dates only and programmes change often, but you can be sure something exciting is going on during your visit.

## VEHICLES

Other modes of transportation available in Main Street, U.S.A. date from the same era as the trains. These vehicles are not genuine antiques, but they are authentically re-created by master craftsmen. Among them are horse-drawn streetcars pulled by patient Percherons, an early double-decker omnibus, a chauffeured limousine, a fire truck and a police wagon. Guests can queue up in Town Square for a brief ride to Central Plaza in whichever vehicle is running. But don't be deceived by Main Street Motors, which in spite of its name and the reconditioned genuine vintage car on display inside, sells souvenirs based on Disney and animated films.

© Disney

FUENTE DEL OR

RESTAURANTE

# Frontierland

©DISNEY

**This is the largest of the five lands, distinguished by a Wild West theme, large expanses of water, and a spectacular Arizona-style landscape. Here is one of the most exciting attractions of the Disneyland® Park, Big Thunder Mountain, and two different kinds of boat trip are offered. Like Main Street, U.S.A.®, Frontierland has a clear architectural theme, based on an imaginary Wild West town of the late 1800s called Thunder Mesa. If parts of Frontierland look surprisingly authentic, that is because they are. Disney Imagineers® collected genuine artefacts from many states in the US, and transported them here for special effect.**

There is something for everyone here. Even if you are not a Wild West enthusiast, you will almost certainly be impressed by the drama of this artificial landscape, created from unpromising, flat terrain. The Disney Imagineers excelled themselves here, re-creating the American West to such an extent that, looking at the wild canyons and ochre sandstone monoliths, you will imagine yourself travelling through the Rocky Mountains. Pioneer fever will no doubt grip you as you step into the Lucky Nugget Saloon to munch some Tex-Mex and watch a real French cancan show!

You can approach Frontierland from several directions. The usual way is from Central Plaza, through Fort Comstock. If you go anticlockwise, you approach Frontierland from Adventureland, and watch how the pirate scene fades to cowboys and Indians. You can also come by train (clockwise round Disneyland Park). On the way between Frontierland Depot and Main Street Station, trains pass through Grand Canyon Diorama (► 66–67).

© Disney

## BIG THUNDER MOUNTAIN *(FASTPASS®)*

The most exciting and conspicuous attraction in Frontierland, and one of the best in Disneyland® Park. It may take a while to pluck up the courage to visit this ride, so wild are the screams from those riding it. But do not miss this experience. It is reached by taking a roller-coaster ride aboard a runaway mine train. The track passes through a reconstructed landscape, similar to that found in Arizona or Utah, particularly around Monument Valley. The rocky set rises to 36m (118ft), and pains have been taken to 'age' the mine buildings by staining, bleaching and rusting.

The ride is certainly wilder than at Orlando. What makes it so good is its mystery factor. Unlike most roller-coasters, the runaway mine train at Big Thunder Mountain is unpredictable and once the train goes into the mine workings anything can happen.

Even the queuing is creatively arranged here – the tightly coiled lines shuffle steadily through the Big Thunder Mountain Mining Company's headquarters. Tension builds up as the point of no return is reached. The train pulls away, then plunges into a shaft and the caverns of the mine workings, full of stalactites and glowing bats' eyes. Hurtling through a mining camp and a pine forest, where possoms swing from the branches, the train dives into a dynamite explosion. The roof caves in, briefly revealing huge veins of gold. The train plunges on, this time facing a new danger from the flooding river, which is washing away part of the track. Eventually the exhilarated passengers are brought safely back to base, eager to do it all again. Children under three (or below 1.02m/3.3ft in height) are not allowed to go on the ride; nor should you attempt it if you are pregnant, or have neck or back problems.

© Disney

**CRITTER CORRAL**
Enclosure of a typical Western ranch near Frontierland Depot (railway station) where visitors can see and pet some real animals.

## FORT COMSTOCK AND LEGENDS OF THE WILD WEST

Guarding the main entrance to Frontierland, Fort Comstock is a replica of the sort of log stockade constructed by early pioneers as a defence against Indian attack. Inside, a series of picturesque scenes depict life in the American West with the help of legendary types of characters immortalized in famous westerns; there is the gold prospector called 'Forty-Niner', because of the 1849 Gold Rush, the outlaw and the lawman, as well as the larger-than-life characters, Buffalo Bill and Davy Crockett.

© Dis

The Indian Camp outside gives a vivid account of the Native Americans' traditional way of life and visitors can admire authentic Cheyenne handicraft. The tour also offers a splendid overall view of Frontierland and the opportunity to meet a real Cheyenne Indian chief.

## GRAND CANYON DIORAMA

Although this attraction is located within Frontierland, it can only be seen from the Disneyland Railroad (trains depart regularly from Main Street, U.S.A., Frontierland, Fantasyland and Discoveryland stations).

Trains enter an 80m (262ft) tunnel, in which the scenery of the Grand Canyon is re-created, subtly lit to give the impression that the journey along the canyon rim takes not just a few minutes, but an entire day from sunrise to sunset. Guests first encounter ancient Indian cliff dwellings hollowed from the canyon walls, and then a forest in which a herd of deer is grazing. Other wildlife can be seen, too: a fox stalking a pack rat; a rattlesnake coiled on a ledge; raccoons and squirrels; and a cougar and her cubs by a cave. A thunderstorm gathers and, as a rainbow forms, antelope descend into the canyon. The diorama consists of a huge mural, with many animals and species of vegetation. Lighting, music and sound effects all play a part. As the train emerges from the tunnel passengers find they have reached the Rivers of the Far West, with Big Thunder Mountain beyond.

© Disney

### PHANTOM MANOR

The eerie, ramshackle mansion of Phantom Manor was built by one of Thunder Mesa's early settlers, who became rich during the Gold Rush. But tragedy struck when his only daughter disappeared on her wedding day. The house was left empty and fell into decay – but isn't that a candle inside?

Guests bound for Phantom Manor are ushered into a strange circular room by sinister hosts. The doors shut and the walls change shape. Those innocent-looking pictures take on horrifying new dimensions as the floor stretches. Guests then descend to

© Disney

board a 'Doom Buggy' for the journey through the house. Mocking laughter, beating door-knockers, creaking hinges, and a clock tolling 13 start the mystery tour. A ghostly bride appears sobbing at intervals, while a medium's head is visible in a crystal ball. One of the best special effects is the holograms, which are used for the wedding feast. Guests dance and fade, and a parade of ghosts, ghouls and skeletons follows before the passengers are released from their ordeal.

### POCAHONTAS INDIAN VILLAGE

This imaginative playground is the perfect place to park young children while you are queuing for rides.

© Disney

### RIVER ROGUE KEELBOATS

These boats are modelled on the ones used in a Disney television film called *Davy Crockett and the River Pirates*. They are diesel-powered, 12m (40ft) long and hold about 40 passengers each. The keelboats weave in and out, and you may find yourself perilously close to the rocks at some point. The keelboats leave from a dock at Smuggler's Cove (in summer only, subject to weather conditions).

### RUSTLER ROUNDUP SHOOTIN' GALLERY

This is fun. Instead of bullets, the guns fire electronic impulses at a Wild West scene containing 74 animated targets: among them cacti, a windmill and a dynamite shack. (The only human one is a peeping Tom.) If you hit them, all kinds of things happen. There is a charge for this attraction to prevent people from hogging the guns all day.

© Disney

© Disney

### THUNDER MESA RIVERBOAT LANDING (PADDLEWHEEL RIVERBOAT)

The landscaping and detailing of the sections of the Rivers of the Far West make the paddlewheel riverboat trip (summer only) round Big Thunder Mountain quite an adventure. On the way you will see Smuggler's Cove; Wilderness Island, a green oasis where Joe sleeps in a rocking-chair, his dog barking at passing boats; Settlers' Landing, a dry dock with supplies for homesteaders; an abandoned wagon with two skeletal oxen in the sand; and Geyser Plateau, where steaming, bubbling, mineral-rich water jets over the dinosaur bones. The scenery evokes a Wild West landscape, with its grand geological formations (rock bridges and canyons) and high desert plateaux known as mesas.

From Thunder Mesa Riverboat Landing near the Silver Spur Steakhouse visitors take the *Molly Brown* riverboat. It is an authentic reconstruction of the paddlewheel riverboats that plied the Mississippi and Sacramento rivers at the time of the Gold Rush and was built specifically for Disneyland® Park. The vessel is fitted with mahogany and brass, teak decks and comfortable upholstery. The boat carries about 400 passengers, and the voyage lasts around 15 minutes.

# Adventureland

© Disney

©DISNEY

This is one of the most attractive parts of Disneyland® Park. In contrast to Frontierland, here there is no geographic unity since the inspiration of the Disney Imagineers® is drawn from three continents – the islands of the Caribbean, the African desert and the Asian jungle. Yet Adventureland is pleasantly landscaped in a natural style, with water, islands, rocks and lots of vegetation, including a bamboo grove. In addition, it has two of the most popular rides, a collection of genuinely interesting shops in its North African bazaar, and several of the nicest eating places. In all, it has a lot going for it, and should appeal to any age group.

One of the two main attractions, Pirates of the Caribbean, is complex and technically sophisticated – yet Adventureland as a whole has an air of innocence about it in keeping with the original spirit of Disney. Its pleasures are simpler than much of Disneyland Park – climbing treehouses, walking wobbly bridges, exploring caves. The central physical feature is Adventure Isle, a moated double-island connected by two exciting bridges. Skilful landscaping gives this area the impression of being larger than it really is. Elements from three well-known Disney movies are incorporated into the themes here: *Peter Pan*, *Treasure Island* and *Swiss Family Robinson*.

© Disney

## ADVENTURE ISLE

The north section of Adventure Isle is given over to a pirate theme. The Jolly Roger flies by the lookout tower on Spyglass Hill. Below is Ben Gunn's Cave, with six different entrances: Dead Man's Maze, Davy Jones's Locker, and so on, leading to mysterious passages haunted by bats and skeletons. Waterfalls hurtle past gaps in the skull-shaped rock. Captain Hook's Pirate Ship is moored in the cove nearby, and you can walk over the top deck to spy out the land. Down below, light snacks are served from the galley. At night Skull Rock and the waterfalls are eerily illuminated. Pirates' Beach is a children's play area (maximum height 1.4m/5ft).

## ALADDIN'S ENCHANTED WORLD (LE PASSAGE ENCHANTÉ D'ALADDIN)

Situated in Adventureland's Bazaar, this attraction brings to life the enchanted city of Aladdin's tales. As you walk through a setting inspired by the Arabian Nights, scenes from Aladdin appear before your eyes, with animated figures and special light and sound effects that will transport your imagination from the city of Agrabah to the Cave of Wonders where the magic lamp lies hidden.

## INDIANA JONES™ AND THE TEMPLE OF PERIL (FASTPASS®)

A daring high-speed roller coaster ride culminating in a thrilling loop-the-loop. We all know the fearless archaeologist who appears in several exciting films. The setting here is an ancient temple full of hidden treasures, in a wild, untamed jungle. Aboard a goldmine cart you begin a perilous chase up, over and under the mine site, past ancient statues and teetering columns.

© Disney

© Disney

## PIRATES OF THE CARIBBEAN

One of the block-busting attractions of the Disneyland® Park, a must for everyone. There are similar attractions at the other Disney® Parks, too, but here the latest Audio-Animatronics® technology gives an even wider range of special effects. As you make your way through the rocky grotto to the boats

© Disney

you can hear roistering buccaneers singing their favourite song. You are about to embark on a time-travel adventure, harking back to a 17th-century scene in the West Indies, where palms wave and the air is warm and balmy. The boat sets off through the moonlit Blue Lagoon and gradually the sounds of distant gunfire grow louder; a fortress is being shelled by a pirate ship. Pirates are attempting to scale the walls, daggers clutched between their teeth. The boat then passes inside the fortress. The ride is so packed with detailed scenery that it is hard to take everything in amid the general plunder and mayhem. Passengers can buy pirate souvenirs afterwards in Le Coffre du Capitaine.

As many as 124 Audio-Animatronics® figures are used, including animals. Some of the animated scenes are highly naturalistic and sophisticated: full of sword-fights, facial gestures and so on. The weapons are authentic replicas of 16th- and 17th-century pieces. The dialogue is mostly in colloquial French, but clues are almost entirely visual, so there is no great loss of enjoyment for non-French speakers. This ride is so action-packed that you could certainly do it more than once. Prepare for a few splashes on the way.

## SWISS FAMILY ROBINSON TREEHOUSE (LA CABANE DES ROBINSON)

Prominent on Adventure Isle is a strange-looking artificial banyan (fig) tree, rising 28m (92ft). In its branches, bearing 300,000 leaves and 50,000 flowers, is the ultimate treehouse, where the resourceful Robinson family have made a home from shipwrecked timbers. Wooden stairways lead to rooms, while by the roots of the tree is le Ventre de la Terre, where supplies from the wreck are stored behind bamboo bars. (The wreck can be seen under the bridge.)

© Disney

# Fantasyland

©DISNEY

**When you reach the neat gardens and fountains of Central Plaza, you can see straight ahead of you the mysterious gilded pinnacles of a truly fantastic castle, and the drawbridge is down, just waiting for you to cross. Sleeping Beauty Castle is the main landmark of Disneyland® Park. It is slap in the centre and unmissable, so it is always a good place to meet. Its spires, visible from most sections of the Park, wil orientate you if you get lost.**

If you approach Fantasyland from Central Plaza when the live show is on at the open-air Théâtre du Château at the foot of the castle, take time to watch as it will put you and your children in the right mood for the fairytale world you are about to enter. You would be surprised how many adults enjoy themselves watching Winnie the Pooh and Friends, Too!. These shows are renewed regularly but are always very popular. Other live shows take place on Fantasy Festival Stage, near Fantasyland Station. Most of Fantasyland's attractions are designed for younger guests; teenagers may find Dumbo the Flying Elephant a little beneath their dignity. At first, that is. The theme of Fantasyland, as its name suggests, is the world of fairy-tales: witches and dwarfs, princes and princesses, ginger-bread houses and magic wishing wells. The European origin of these fairy-tales is heavily emphasized. Architecture ranges from quaint, Bavarian-looking cottages to the ambitious medieval whimsy of the castle itself.

Several of the attractions are similar in type: short rides through enclosed spaces, during which a fairy story is unfurled with many elaborate sets and moving figures. The characters are deliberately based on Disney animated films. There is no attempt to make them look like 'real people'. Queues for these attractions are often lengthy. Pinocchio's Fantastic Journey or Peter Pan's Flight are

© Disney

difficult to follow if you are not familiar with the stories, though you can still enjoy the rides. Other attractions are of the fairground variety – in the form of classic merry-go-rounds and a few mild G-forces. If you know other Disney® Parks you will probably remember the block-busting and eternally popular 'it's a small world', here given more elaboration.

Newer attractions include the hedge maze of Alice's Curious Labyrinth – again, a strongly European feature, and Le Pays des Contes de Fées (Fairytale Land).

Elsewhere in Fantasyland there are many shops selling toys and sweets, and also lots of fairy-tale eating places (designed mostly with children in mind), including one of the few restaurants in the Park with French cuisine, Auberge de Cendrillon. You can reach Fantasyland by the Disneyland Railroad, but after that you must use your feet.

© Disney

### ALICE'S CURIOUS LABYRINTH

Based, of course, on *Alice in Wonderland*, this maze of clipped cypress and ivy hedges is 366m (1,200ft) long. You will pass characters and scenes from Alice: the Cheshire Cat, which rolls its eyes and twitches its tail, a blue caterpillar calmly smoking a hookah, strange birds and the choleric Queen of Hearts advocating decapitation at every turn. Eventually you reach a small purple castle, full of optical illusions. The jumping fountains transfix passers-by; arcs of water leap from pool to pool round the edge of the maze. The designs for some parts of this attraction are unusual and keep children amused for quite some time.

### CASEY JR – LE PETIT TRAIN DU CIRQUE

Straight out of the Disney classic *Dumbo,* this seasonal circus train rides up and down small hills and over bridges as it jerks its passengers swiftly round the miniature sets of Storybook Land (► 85). A gentle ride for anyone over the age of one.

## THE DRAGON'S DEN (LA TANIÈRE DU DRAGON)

Chained by the neck in a dark cave of bubbling pools and stalactites is a leathery grey dragon, wonderfully terrifying. It makes gentle snorings and twitchings, then flashes its red eyes and gives fierce roars, smoke pouring from its nostrils. Its tail lashes in the water, while the wings move and claws tense. It is one of the most remarkable and sophisticated pieces of Audio-Animatronics® technology in the Disneyland® Park. You can reach its lair from the mysterious shop called Merlin l'Enchanteur, carved into the rock of the castle.

© Disney

## DUMBO THE FLYING ELEPHANT

The long queues for this ride testify to the popular appeal of this simple roundabout for young children. You can even control the height at which your elephant flies.

## 'IT'S A SMALL WORLD'

As with similar attractions at Tokyo, Orlando and Anaheim, this is a very popular and elaborate attraction. In Disneyland® Park it is a fantastic amalgam of many different architectural landmarks, ranging from Big Ben to the Leaning Tower of Pisa. The set is constructed in miniature. Every quarter of an hour a parade of animated figures troops around the base of the clocktower, and many exciting things happen before you are eventually told what time it is. Guests take a ride in canal boats past a gathering of Audio-Animatronics® 'children' from all parts of the globe. Norwegian figure-skaters give way to leprechauns, London's Beefeaters, Flamenco dancers, Balinese fan-dancers and the like. It is a saccharine show, but the technical effects are none the less impressive. There are nearly 280 different figures, representing a phenomenal effort by the Disney costume department.

© Disney

© Disney

### LANCELOT'S CAROUSEL (LE CARROUSEL DE LANCELOT)

A classic merry-go-round, with 86 ornate, medieval war horses trotting through fairy-tale scenes. A gentle ride.

### MAD HATTER'S TEACUPS

A pleasantly loony whirl in 18 giant teacups, placed on a roundabout, resulting in a bewildering pirouette of motion. You control the speed using a steering wheel.

### PETER PAN'S FLIGHT (*FASTPASS®*)

Pirate galleons 'sail' over the rooftops of London to Neverland, giving an illusion of flight. A delightful journey for day-dreamers of all ages.

### PINOCCHIO'S FANTASTIC JOURNEY

Based on the story told by Carlo Collodi. The cars pass from Alpine landscapes into dangers and temptations, and then emerge back in Geppetto's shop, where the clockwork toys spring to life.

## SLEEPING BEAUTY CASTLE

This is the archetypal interpretation of a castle – one we instantly recognize from the pages of any storybook, or from early Disney movies, such as the animated classic *Sleeping Beauty*.

The design is loosely based on the architecture of Normandy's famous abbey-castle of Mont-St-Michel, and on illustrations from a 17th-century edition of *Les Très Riches Heures du Duc de Berry*. The building rises 45.5m (149ft) above the moat. A technique known as 'forced perspective' has

© Disney

been employed, to give an illusion of even greater height. The pink walls are topped by 16 whimsical ornamental turrets of subtle, sea-blue tiles. Pennants, weather vanes and golden finials adorn the roofline; creepers hang from the walls; and enticing stairways lead to the central tower. Visitors can enter the castle by the drawbridge, or from the side by the wishing well (Le Puits Magique); don't forget to wish. Once inside, turn and look up at the front window – and

© Disney

wait a few seconds. Magically, its design will transform from two doves into a rose. This is a 'polage window', and it works by means of a rotating filter. Upstairs, in la Galerie de la Belle au Bois Dormant (Sleeping Beauty's Gallery) there is an exhibition of hand-woven Aubusson tapestries, colourful stained-glass windows made by English craftsmen and illuminated manuscripts depicting the famous story of *Sleeping Beauty*. From the balcony, the view over Fantasyland is splendid.

## SNOW WHITE AND THE SEVEN DWARFS (BLANCHE-NEIGE ET LES SEPT NAINS)

Climb aboard the diamond-mine cars outside the Dwarfs' cottage, and set off through this German fairy-tale, on which Walt Disney based one of his most successful animated films. The wicked queen does her stuff with the mirror and the poisoned apple, and Prince Charming appears at the end.

© Disney

## STORYBOOK LAND (LE PAYS DES COUTES DE FÉES)

Miniature scenes from European fairy-tales unfold slowly as children of all ages take a canal cruise through familiar landscapes that re-create the magical appeal of delightful tales such as *Hansel and Gretel*, the *Little Mermaid* and *Beauty and the Beast*. But there is more...the imposing Mount Olympus where Greek gods once lived, Aladdin's cave and the legend of King Arthur.

## Discoveryland

This European version of Tomorrowland also looks back at the great inventors of the past. Here, in France, Jules Verne is given a prominent role; H G Wells and Leonardo da Vinci are also featured.

©DISNEY

© Disney

Special effects form the basis of the Videopolis show and Honey, I Shrunk the Audience attraction. Elsewhere, you will travel through time and space in Discoveryland, and even to the bottom of the ocean in Captain Nemo's submarine (Les Mystères du Nautilus). Certain attractions involve long queues, particularly Star Tours and Space Mountain: Mission 2, while the recently added Buzz Lightyear's Laser Blast is sure to pull in the crowds. Budget-conscious visitors should be aware that the video games arcades (Alpha and Beta) and the interactive computer games of L'Astroport Services Interstellaires (Star Tours Post-Show) are chargeable.

If, as many people do, you tackle the Disneyland® Park clockwise, this is the last land you will come to, and psychologically it feels as though it should be. The architecture is futuristic, with lights and flashing lasers.

© Disney

### AUTOPIA

This is a popular attraction, consisting of a ride in a 'Car of the Future' through 'Solaria', a city of tomorrow. Your car is kept firmly on a specific track, and all you have to do is press the accelerator and steer. There's a minimum height regulation for unaccompanied users (1.32m/4ft 3in). It is closed off-season.

## BUZZ LIGHTYEAR LASER BLAST *(FASTPASS®)*

Opened in April 2006, this exciting interactive adventure is inspired by the Disney-Pixar Animation Studios film *Toy Story 2*. The Evil Emperor Zurg has a fiendish plan to power up his robot invasion army with the batteries stolen from every toy in the universe. Space Ranger Buzz Lightyear calls on all Disneyland® Resort Paris guests to help him foil the Emperor. Aboard a two-seater space cruiser, you take charge of dual laser pistols and a joystick enabling full 360-degree rotation of the vehicle. Your mission is to shoot as many targets as you can during the ride. As you disembark, your point-score indicates your rank, starting at modest Star Cadet level or achieving the supreme accolade of Galactic Hero. Don't forget your souvenir photo to mark the occasion.

## HONEY, I SHRUNK THE AUDIENCE

© Disney

This original attraction, inspired by the two Disney successes *Honey, I Shrunk the Kids* and *Honey, I Blew up the Kid*, opened to great acclaim in 1999. You watch as accident-prone inventor Wayne Szalinski (hero of the two films) demonstrates his shrinking and enlarging machine and commits his biggest blunder – pointing the machine at the audience! From the start you are carefully prepared for the worst as you are given special glasses to wear as you enter the first auditorium, where a multimedia pre-show whets the appetite. You are then ushered into the main auditorium and the action starts, as state-of-the-art special effects create the highly convincing 'shrinking' effect, through 3D visual effects, surround-sound and touch sensations on leg and face. The show reaches its height when young Adam Szalinski picks up the auditorium and the whole theatre starts to shake…

## LES MYSTÈRES DU NAUTILUS

This attraction was inspired by Disney's movie *20,000 Leagues under the Sea* based on Jules Verne's novel. Docked in Discoveryland's lagoon, the *Nautilus* is Captain Nemo's submarine,

the strange universe of an eccentric visionary who plays the organ
at the bottom of the sea. An undersea passage, reached through
a nearby lighthouse, leads to the interior of the submarine.

The tour of the vessel holds a few surprises in store for you,
as well as some spine-chilling sound and light effects. It begins
in the Treasure Room and ends in the Engine Room.

### ORBITRON®

There is nothing new about the basic principle of this ride, but it
certainly looks different. Bronze, copper and brass globes spin on
various axes, the opposite way from the direction of your two-
seater craft, so if you are at maximum height (controlled from
inside) it seems quite fast. Queues can be very long, as there
are only 12 passenger vehicles.

## SPACE MOUNTAIN: MISSION 2 *(FASTPASS®)*

Entirely reprogrammed in 2005, Space Mountain: Mission 2 blasts daring 'exploronauts' far beyond the moon to the outer edges of the universe, encountering comets and supernovas en route. This attraction undoubtedly marks the climax of a visit to the Disneyland® Park. The setting, the sounds and the awe-inspiring darkness, torn by incandescent asteroids, are all designed to make you feel like space pioneers. The exhilarating experience begins long before boarding the rocket ship: while you slowly make your way through the heart of the impressive 36m-high (118ft) 'mountain', you experience a taste of the dangers ahead with meteorites and explosions all around. But the count-down to blast off is ticking away and it is time for the rocket ship to enter the barrel of the 22m-long (72ft) Columbiad Cannon, inspired by Jules Verne's novel *From the Earth to the Moon* published in 1865. The

© Disney

take-off, now from the lower part of the cannon, increases the launch phase by some 40 per cent. Passengers experience acceleration of 14m/s and a G-force of almost 1.3N, before plunging into space on a hair-raising 1km (0.5-mile) journey at a top speed of 70kph (43mph). In its efforts to avoid impending annihilation, the rocket ship makes three complete inversion loops while a sophisticated on-board audio system, with five loudspeakers per seat, adds to the thrills. If you don't want to take the ride, which is extremely intense and has height, age and fitness requirements, you can still gain a vivid idea of this fantastic space journey by walking along the mountain's interior gangways.

### STAR TOURS *(FASTPASS®)*

© Disney

This exciting attraction draws on the themes and special effects used in George Lucas's epic adventure, *Star Wars*. As much excitement is created by the build-up as by the ride itself. The sci-fi 'business' before you are actually strapped into your spacecraft, when visitors can

watch friendly droids working, is all part of the fun, and certainly takes tedium out of queuing. The attraction is based on a popular comic theme: the novice driver. This one, unfortunately, is your pilot for the space flight. Fasten your seat-belts. The space craft pitches, rolls and jolts, while on-screen, rapidly moving images suggest you are falling or are on some irrevocable collision course. Eventually, of course, you land safely to be greeted by Rox-N, a clever robot who presents the interactive computer games of

L'Astroport Services Interstellaires (Star Tours Post-Show) in five languages. There is an X-ray detector with videoscreen projection to eliminate minute space creatures. There is also a sophisticated camera which takes your photograph and projects it on a large screen; you can then distort it at will by dragging your finger across the screen. But the most exciting game is Star Course, when would-be pilots try their skill at avoiding obstacles while hurtling through space at high speed.

## VIDEOPOLIS

The airship *Hyperion* marks this pavilion, which houses a large tiered auditorium where visitors can enjoy videos relayed on four giant screens and exhilarating live shows such as *The Legend of the Lion King*. The Café Hyperion offers a good view of the stage, so you can munch hamburgers and hotdogs while you watch. Unearthly special effects are created by lasers.

© Disney

# Walt Disney Studios® Park

**Walt Disney Studios® Park, opened 10 years after Disneyland® Park, is designed to take its guests to the very source of the Disney magic, on a thrilling interactive journey behind the scenes to discover some of the secrets of Disney animation, to marvel at special effects, to witness spectacular stunts and take part in a live television broadcast. And, anything can happen when Mickey takes over as cameraman! Lights on, take one!**

© Disney

The park is divided into four Production Zones based on a real studio and includes 10 attractions and several shops and restaurants. There is also endless entertainment called 'Streetmosphere': actors, musicians and characters adding to the atmosphere of a real working film studio. Walt Disney Studios Park is generally less crowded than Disneyland Park. Be sure to catch the shows.

# Front Lot

**Beyond the Park's gates, the inviting courtyard shaded by palm trees with a fountain in its centre (could it be Mickey in disguise?!) reveals none of the excitement that lies ahead.**

© Disney

The focal point of this area, known as 'Front Lot' in cinema jargon, is undoubtedly the 33m-high (108ft) water tower topped by Mickey's famous pair of black ears. Originally used to fight fires, such towers became the symbol of a Hollywood film studio; this one was modelled on the water tower erected near the entrance to the Disney Studios in Burbank, California in 1939. And as you might expect, there is a definite 1930s air about the place. Beyond the courtyard lies the entrance to Disney Studio 1.

## DISNEY STUDIO 1

Here you step straight into the glaring lights of a Hollywood film set, Hollywood Boulevard, packed with movie props and lined with shops and a restaurant, where guests become part of the action! Studio 1 is a veiled reference to Walt Disney's studios in Los Angeles, which were the birthplace of the Mickey Mouse animated shorts and of Disney's first full-length animated film, *Snow White and the Seven Dwarfs*. Some of the sets are inspired by buildings that actually existed, others help to re-create the atmosphere of Hollywood during the first half of the 20th century.

© Disney

# Backlot

**According to studio jargon, this area is usually not on show...this is where the tricks of the trade are developed, perfected and eventually filmed, all very hush-hush and definitely out of bounds, but not at Walt Disney Studios® Park!**

© Disney

### ARMAGEDDON, SPECIAL EFFECTS

This attraction takes its name from the science-fiction film featuring the Mir space station. The pre-show area pays tribute to the inventor of special effects, Frenchman George Méliès, and puts you in the mood for what's in store! Once you step on board the space station, the mounting suspense becomes almost unbearable as all sorts of apocalyptic things happen...or do they?

© Disney

Could it be that those visual and sound effects are more real than reality itself? Well the thrill is certainly real enough anyway, so enjoy it!

### MOTEURS...ACTION! STUNT SHOW SPECTACULAR®

This is what every James Bond fan would like to see...a live stunt show! And this is exactly what Walt Disney Studios Park is offering you – a breathtaking spectacular staged up to five times a day in a 3,000-seat outdoor arena. The scene is a seaside village in southern France, the action: a live shooting of various stunts with purpose-designed powerful cars, motorcycles and jet skis and then you get a chance to see it all again...on screen!

### ROCK'N'ROLLER COASTER STARRING AEROSMITH

A spine-chilling ride (height restriction) with a difference! It has the speed, the acceleration, the loops, the turns, the drops that you'd expect...but it also has the music and stunning visual effects.

# Toon Studio®

**This is the temple of the art of animation for which the name of Disney became famous worldwide. Five attractions, including exhibits and shows, are devoted to the evolution of animation from its European origins to the most sophisticated feature-length animated pictures of our time.**

### ANIMAGIQUE®

Staged in a 1,100-seat theatre, this 'black-light' show using giant fluorescent puppets, ultra-violet light and special effects is partly orchestrated by Donald Duck! Characters from your favourite Disney animated pictures (Mickey, Donald, Pinocchio, the pink elephants, the whale…) come to life in this three-dimensional animated show…as if by magic!

© Disney

### ART OF DISNEY ANIMATION®

Creating the illusion of motion is a dream that goes back to prehistoric man. Many pioneers have tried to make this dream come true and the pre-show film pays homage to them. The pre-show area also displays artefacts, some of them unique, such as the multi-plane camera developed by Walt Disney in the 1930s to add depth to animated images by allowing various parts of the same picture to be animated separately. And why not have a go yourself at the 'persistence of vision' apparatus?

The attraction itself, a sequence which takes place in three successive rooms, includes a film with highlights from Disney's animated classics to whet your appetite for what follows in the second room, Drawn to Animation. There, you see a demonstration of how it is done by a Disney artist with the help of Mushu, the little red dragon from the film *Mulan*. After this, character animation will no longer hold any secrets and you will be

© Disney

given a chance to try your newly acquired skill at the interactive play stations located in the last room.

## CARS AND CRUSH

These attractions, based on the hit movies *Finding Nemo* and *Cars*, opened in 2007. Guests board Crush's Coaster and descend into Nemo's world with all the effects the latest technology can bring. All age-groups can cllimb onto the spinning Cars Race Rally ride which follows the famous Route 66. Characters from the film cheer drivers on.

## FLYING CARPETS OVER AGRABAH®

Hang on to your magic carpet as you're whirled round a giant magic lamp and let your imagination take flight into a far-off land where illusion and reality become mixed up.

# Production Courtyard®

A statue of Charlie Chaplin as he appeared in *City Lights*, one of his most moving films, marks the entrance to this part of Walt Disney Studios® Park. This is the hub, the place where it all happens, where the spectators' dream becomes reality...on screen!

## CINÉMAGIQUE

This show is a tribute to the magic appeal of European and US cinema over the past hundred years. Featuring a selection of the most exciting film excerpts as well as a review of the actors and actresses who are now part of the legend, it invites guests to relive cinema's greatest moments. Inside the 1,100-seat theatre, do not be deceived by the 1930s décor. You are about to experience the powerful effect of the latest technology and witness an exciting fusion of fiction and reality!

## STUDIO TRAM TOUR®: BEHIND THE MAGIC

When you climb aboard the studio tram you are taken on a popular fun-packed tour backstage. See film sets, props, costumes and vehicles from some of your favourite movies, and learn how some of the special effects are created. But there is one mighty detail that will make all the difference to your flow of adrenalin: your tram will take a dramatic detour via Catastrophe Canyon® and from then on you find yourself at the heart of the special-effect shooting of a series of hair-raising disasters!

## THE TWILIGHT ZONE TOWER OF TERROR™

This new attraction, open in Spring 2008, features an exciting 13-floor elevator drop.

## WALT DISNEY TELEVISION STUDIOS

This is home to the Disney Channel France and it is the very first time that a television network has been based inside a Disney® Park! A tour guide shows you round the Transmission Centre, from which programmes are broadcast live throughout France six days a week. How about watching yourself appear on TV, or designing your very own CyberSpace roller-coaster? Then check it out on the simulator, and wish you'd chosen a gentler ride.

# Excursions

If your aim is to see a bit more of France during your visit to Disneyland® Resort Paris, there is plenty to do for all the family without having to travel too far. Shoppers will enthuse over the huge Val d' Europe complex on the doorstep of Disneyland Resort Paris. At La Vallée Shopping Village you can find all the latest designer labels – many at reduced prices.

And of course, a short ride takes you into Paris with its fantastic array of smart shops, grand department stores and interesting markets, where you can explore dozens of galleries, museums and famous sights.

In the countryside around Disneyland Resort Paris are several stunning châteaux, some very well known, such as Versailles and Fontainebleau, and other lesser-known gems.

# Historic Châteaux

The Île de France, Paris's green belt, is well known for its splendid châteaux and great forests. An hour's drive southwards from Disneyland® Resort Paris will enable you to visit the architectural gems of Fontainebleu and Vaux-le-Vicomte and to explore one of the finest forests in the region. Just to the southwest of Paris is the huge château of Versailles, while on the eastern outskirts of the capital stands the formidable castle of Vicennes.

## FONTAINEBLEAU, CHÂTEAU DE

The massive and beautiful château is the main draw, but the great hunting forest that surrounds the town provides a welcome retreat for Parisians. It is an excellent place for picnics, walking, cycling and riding, but is very busy at weekends. As the name suggests, a fountain or spring, now in the Jardin Anglais, is at the origin of this splendid royal residence, which started out as a hunting pavilion in

the heart of the forest. The magnificent apartments were transformed from medieval to Renaissance splendour by François I in the 16th century, and later kings also left their mark.

The opulence of the décor is astonishing, especially the ceilings. The imposing horseshoe staircase decorating the main façade was the scene of Napoleon I's moving farewell to his faithful guard in 1814. In the grounds is the Etang des Carpes (carp pool) with a lovely pavilion at its centre and farther on the formal French gardens.

**www.**musee-chateau-fontainebleau.fr

✉ 77300 Fontainebleau, 63km (39 miles) south of Disneyland® Resort Paris
☎ 01 60 71 50 70 🕒 Wed–Mon 9.30–5 (6 Jun–Sep). Closed 1 Jan, 1 May, 25 Dec ✋ Moderate 🍴 Picnics allowed in the park but not gardens 🚉 Gare de Lyon to Fontainebleau-Avon, then bus A or B ❓ Guided tour, shops

## VAUX-LE-VICOMTE, CHÂTEAU DE

Compared with Fontainebleau or Versailles, this château is small, but its moderate size seems only to enhance its attractiveness and means it can more easily be appreciated and enjoyed in a single visit. The interior has many features and fine antiques, but the grounds are most impressive: illusory vistas, neat topiary, canals and terraced parterres. In the stables is a museum (Musée des Equipages) devoted to horse-drawn carriages. Fountains play on alternate Saturdays in summer and candlelit tours are popular.

The château has an interesting story. It was built by the ambitious politician Nicolas Fouquet, in 1656: Le Vau was the architect, Le Nôtre designed its lovely gardens, and Le Brun supervised the interior. After his gorgeous château was completed in 1661, Fouquet made the disastrous mistake of inviting Louis XIV to dinner, to impress him. The king was impressed, so much so that he seethed with jealousy and fury at this social upstart. Fouquet was arrested on a trumped-up charge and his possessions were seized by the king, who commissioned the very same artists to upstage Vaux-le-Vicomte with an even more ambitious project – Versailles.

**www.**vaux-le-vicomte.com

✉ Domaine de Vaux-le-Vicomte, 77950, 45km (28 miles) south of Disneyland® Resort Paris ☎ 01 64 14 41 90 🕐 Mid-Mar to mid-Nov Mon–Fri 10–1, 2–6, Sat–Sun 10–6 👋 Expensive 🍴 Cafeteria (€) 🚆 Gare de Lyon to Melun then taxi; shuttle bus at weekends/public hols ❓ Shops

## VERSAILLES, CHÂTEAU DE

Versailles is the ultimate symbol of French grandeur, and the backdrop to the death of the monarchy. In 1661, when Louis XIV announced his intention of moving his court to this deserted swamp, it was to create a royal residence, seat of government and home to French nobility. Building continued until his death in 1715, by which time the 100ha (247-acre) park had been tamed to perfection by landscape garden designer André Le Nôtre. Hundreds of statues, follies and fountains, and the royal retreats of the Grand and Petit Trianon relieve the formal symmetry, while rowing boats, bicycles and a minitrain now offer a diversion from history. The castle is huge (680m/2,230ft long) and it is impossible to see everything in the course of one visit. Aim for the first floor with the Grands Appartements (State Apartments), which include the staggeringly ornate Hall of Mirrors. The Petits Appartements display France's most priceless examples of 18th-century

decoration and may be visited by guided tour only.
**www.**chateauversailles.fr

✉ Château de Versailles, 78000 Versailles, 20km (12.5 miles southwest of
Paris ☎ 01 30 83 78 00 🕐 Château: Tue–Sun 9–5.30 (6.30 in summer).
Parc: 7–5.30 (up to 9 depending on season) 🖐 Moderate 🍴 Café (€);
restaurant (€€) 🚉 Gare St-Lazare to Versailles Rive Droit ❓ Guided
tours, shops

## VINCENNES, CHÂTEAU DE

This austere castle, on the eastern outskirts of Paris, was a royal residence from the Middle Ages to the mid-17th century. Inside the defensive wall there are in fact two castles: the 50m-high (164ft) keep built in the 14th century; and the two classical pavilions (Le Pavilion du Reine and Le Pavilion du Roi) built by Le Vau for Cardinal Mazarin in 1652.

**www.**chateau-vincennes.com

✉ Avenue de Paris, 94300 Vincennes, 6km (4 miles) east of Paris

☎ 01 48 08 31 20

🕐 Daily 10–noon, 1–5 (6 in summer). Closed 1 May, 1 Nov, 11 Nov, 25 Dec ✋ Inexpensive

🚇 Porte de Vincennes

❓ Guided tours, shops

**VAL D'EUROPE**
**If you need a change of scene from the Disney universe, this purpose-built development just one stop up the RER Line A towards Paris is well worth a visit.**

A couple of minutes' walk from the RER station stands a huge glass-and-metal complex offering shopping, eating and entertainment. The International Shopping Centre is a double-decker indoor mall incorporating an Auchan hypermarket, plus around 130 separate shops selling a wide range of clothing, electronics, housewares, sports goods and more.

Beyond it lies an attractively designed 'outlet shopping village' called La Vallée, consisting of over 70 designer boutiques selling previous-season and end-of-line stock at prices discounted by up to a third. Well-known international labels include Armani, Burberry, Charles Tyrwhitt, Cacherel etc. There are plenty of eating places at Val d'Europe, and a branch of the splendid boulangerie/pâtisserie Paul does a brisk trade. The centre is open 7 days a week.

Val d'Europe also has a **Sea Life** aquarium displaying a fascinating world of exotic marine creatures in over 30 separate tanks. You can walk through a 360-degree underwater tunnel, and enjoy close encounters with giant sting-rays in the touch-pools. It runs energetic breeding and conservation programmes to protect endangered species such as sea horses and sharks, and campaigns to draw attention to the threat of overfishing in the world's oceans.

### Sea Life Val d'Europe

✉ Centre Commercial Val d'Europe 14, cours du Danube, Serris 77711, Marne-la-Vallée ☎ 01 60 42 33 66 🕐 Daily 10–5.30 💷 Moderate
🚇 RER Line A Val d'Europe ❓ Free parking, shop

# Paris

With so much to see in Paris, if you are only making a short visit, it is worth deciding in advance what you really want to see. For splendid city views, head for the Eiffel Tower, the Pompidou Centre or Montmartre's Sacré-Coeur. For art lovers, the Louvre, the Musée d'Orsay and the Musée Rodin stand out among a rich store of museums and galleries. For spectacular churches, Notre-Dame and Sacré-Coeur are essential viewing.

For shopping, don't miss the area around Faubourg-St-Honoré and the Champs-Élysées. For a leisurely taste of traditional Paris, take a boat trip down the River Seine.

## CENTRE GEORGES POMPIDOU

More than a mere landmark in the extensive face-lift that Paris has undergone since the 1970s, the high-tech Centre Georges Pompidou (known to Parisians as Beaubourg) is a hive of changing cultural activity. Contemporary art, architecture, design, photography, theatre, cinema and dance are all represented, while the lofty structure itself offers exceptional views over central Paris. Take the transparent escalator tubes for a bird's-eye view of the piazza where jugglers, artists, musicians and portrait artists strut their stuff in front of the teeming crowds.

**www.**centrepompidou.fr

✉ Rue Rambuteau, 75004 ☎ 01 44 78 12 33

🕐 Wed–Mon 11–10. Museum and exhibits 11–9; Brancusi Workshop Mon–Fri 2–6; Library Mon, Wed–Fri noon–10, Sat, Sun 11–10 🚇 Permanent collections inexpensive; full ticket expensive 🍴 Restaurant (€€); café (€); snack bar (€) 🚇 Rambuteau, Hôtel de Ville 🚌 38, 47, 75 🚆 RER Line A, B, Châtelet-Les Halles ❓ Frequent lectures, concerts, parallel activities, Atelier des Enfants

## CHAMPS-ÉLYSÉES/ARC DE TRIOMPHE

For most visitors this avenue epitomizes French elegance, but it is also a luxury shopping mall and a dazzling place of entertainment. The Champs-Élysées may be dominated by car showrooms, but plush cinemas, classy shops and one or two fashionable watering holes remain to tempt those who want to see and be seen. The Arc de Triomphe is an image of French national pride, built as a symbol of Napoleon's military strength. There is a wonderful view from the top, 50m (164ft) above street level.

✉ Champs-Élysées, 75008 🍴 Choice of restaurants (€–€€€) 🚇 Charles de Gaulle-Étoile, Georges V, Franklin D Roosevelt, Champs-Élysées-Clémenceau 🚌 32, 42, 73 ❓ Takes around 30 mins to walk from the Arc de Triomphe to place de la Concorde

## JARDIN DU LUXEMBOURG

If you want to get away from the bustle during your trip to Paris these gardens are serene in all weathers and are the epitome of French landscaping. Attractions include shady chestnuts, potted orange and palm trees, lawns and even an experimental fruit garden and

orchard, while fountains, tennis courts, beehives, a puppet theatre and playgrounds offer other distractions. Joggers circle the gardens; sunbathers and bookworms settle into chairs. Statues of the queens of France, artists and writers are dotted about the gardens.

✉ 15 rue de Vaugirard, 75006 (various entries around the park); www.senat.fr ⏰ Daily dawn–dusk 🎟 Free 🍴 Open-air cafés, kiosk restaurant (€–€€) Ⓜ Odéon Ⓡ RER B Luxembourg 🚌 21, 27, 38, 58, 82, 84, 85, 89

## LOUVRE, MUSÉE DU

The world's largest museum was originally a medieval castle. It first took shape as an art gallery under François I, eager to display his Italian loot. The vast collection of some 30,000 exhibits is arranged on four floors of three wings, while beneath the elegant Cour Carrée (courtyard) lie the keep and dungeons of the original medieval fortress. Almost 5,000 years of art are covered, starting with Egyptian antiquities and culminating with European painting up to 1848.

**www.**louvre.fr

✉ 99 rue de Rivoli, 75001 ☎ 01 40 20 53 17 ⏰ Thu–Sun 9–6.45, Mon and Wed 9am–9.45pm 🎟 Moderate until 3pm, inexpensive after 3pm and Sun; free first Sun of every month 🍴 Restaurants and cafés (€–€€) Ⓜ Palais-Royal, Musée du Louvre 🚌 21, 27, 39, 48, 67, 68, 69, 72, 75, 76, 81, 95 ❓ Guided tours and audioguides

## LE MARAIS

The sedate old-world atmosphere of this historic enclave at the heart of the city is unique, full of architectural beauty and cultural diversity. It offers visitors narrow picturesque streets, cafés and bistros, elegant mansions, tiny boutiques and a lively population. Across on the Left Bank you will find the Quartier Latin (Latin Quarter), a trendy student district.

✉ Le Marais  Ⓜ St-Paul, Rambuteau, Hôtel de Ville  🚍 29, 75

## MONTMARTRE/SACRÉ-COEUR

Once the haunt of famous artists, Montmartre retains something of a village atmosphere and the area has become a major tourist attraction. At the top of the village is the basilica of **Sacré-Coeur,** an unmistakable feature of the Paris skyline that magnetizes the crowds arriving either by funicular or via the steep steps of the terraced garden. The view of Paris is breathtaking, stretching for 50km (30 miles).

The dome is the second-highest point in Paris after the Eiffel Tower.

✉ Monmartre, 75018 🚇 Abbesses, Lamarck-Caulaincourt 🚌 Montmartrobus

**Sacré-Coeur**

**www**.sacre-coeur-montmartre.com

✉ Place du Parvis du Sacré-Coeur, 75018 ☎ 01 53 41 89 00 🕐 Basilica: daily 7am–11pm; dome and crypt: 9.15–5.30 ( 7 in summer) 💶 Basilica: free; dome and crypt: inexpensive 🚇 Abbesses (from here, walk along rue Yvonne Le Tac, then take funicular or walk up steps) 🚌 30, 54, 80, 85 Montmartrobus

## NOTRE-DAME/ RIVER SEINE

Notre Dame is a masterpiece of Gothic architecture and one of Paris's most famous landmarks with its 90m (295ft) spire and world-renowned flying buttresses. You can admire it if you take a boat trip along the Seine. There are many splendid monuments to see along the river banks in particular on the Île Saint-Louis and the Île de la Cité, the historic centre of Paris.

### Notre-Dame

✉ Place du Parvis Notre-Dame 75004 ☎ 01 42 34 56 10; crypt 01 43 29 83 51 🕓 Cathedral: daily 9–7.30; closed on some religious feast days. Tower: daily 9.30–7.30, Apr–Sep (also until 11pm, Sat–Sun, Jul–Aug); 10–5.30, rest of year. Treasury: Mon–Sat 9.30–11.30, 1–5.30 ✋ Moderate 🚇 Cité, St-Michel 🚌 24, 47 🚆 RER Lines B and C, St-Michel

### TOUR EIFFEL

Paris's most famous landmark has been towering above the city for more than a hundred years, yet its universal appeal remains constant. Built for the World Exhibition in 1899 by Gustave Eiffel, measuring 324m (1,063ft) in height, it was then the tallest building in the world and an unprecedented technological achievement. Its iron frame weighs 7,000 tonnes and 40 tonnes of paint are used to repaint it every seven years. There are three levels, all accessible by lift or stairs – a breathtaking 1,710 steps to the final stage. The genius of the construction by Eiffel shows in the fact that the tower sways no more than 9cm (3.5in) in high winds. It remained the world's highest structure for more than 40 years.

**www.**tour-eiffel.fr

✉ Champ de Mars, 75007 ☎ 01 44 11 23 23 🕐 Daily 9.30am–11am (stairs 9.30–6.30; dusk in winter), Sep–Jun; 9am–midnight, Jul–Aug (last admission one hour before closing) ♿ Expensive; stairs inexpensive 🍴 Restaurants (€–€€€) Ⓜ Bir-Hakeim 🚌 42, 69, 72, 82, 87 🚆 RER Line C, Champs de Mars, Tour Eiffel

# Index

# Acknowledgements

The Automobile Association would like to thank the following photographers, companies and picture libraries in the preparation of this book.

Abbreviations for the picture credits are as follows – (t) top; (b) bottom; (l) left; (r) right; (c) center; (AA) AA World Travel Library.

**4l** Disneyland Park entrance in Winter, © Disney; **4c** Sleeping Beauty Castle at Sunset, © Disney; **4r** Cabane de Robinson, © Disney; **5l** Domaine de Vaux-le-Vicomte, Paris, AA/B Rieger; **5c** Sleeping Beauty's Castle, © Disney; **5r** Nighttime in Montmartre, AA/P Enticknap; **6/7** Disneyland Park entrance in Winter, © Disney; **10/11** Graphics of Disneyland Park at night, © Disney; **12** Disneyland Park, © Disney; **14/15** Gare de Nord, Paris, AA/C Sawyer; **16** Metro Station, Paris, AA/C Sawyer; **16/17** Bus, Paris, AA/M Jourdan; **18/19** Metro sign, Paris, AA/K Paterson; **22/23** Sleeping Beauty Caste at sunset, © Disney; **26/27** Little Girl with Mickey Mouse Balloon, © Disney; **30** Bust of Walt Disney, © Disney; **32** Adventureland, © Disney; **34** Prince Ali, © Disney; **34/35** Big Thunder Mountain by night, © Disney; **36** Disney characters on Meet and Greet, © Disney; **39** Fastpass logo, © Disney; **46/47** A magic day at Disneyland Paris, © Disney; **49** Sleeping child, © Disney; **50/51** Cabane de Robinson, © Disney; **52** Disneyland Park entrance, © Disney; **53** Disneyland Park logo, © Disney; **54t** Main Street logo, © Disney; **54b** Main Street, USA, © Disney; **55** City Hall, Disney, © Disney; **56t** Libery Arcade, © Disney; **56b** Shopping, Main Street USA, © Disney; **58/59** Wonderful World of Disney Parade, © Disney; **60/61** Wonderful World of Disney Parade, © Disney; **61** Main Street Vehicles, © Disney; **62** Fuente del Oro Restaurant, © Disney; **63** Frontierland logo, © Disney; **64/65** Big Thunder Mountain, © Disney; **66** Cottonwood Creek Ranch, © Disney; **66/67** Chip 'n' Dale in Frontierland, © Disney; **68/69** Phantom Manor, © Disney; **69t** Phantom Manor, © Disney; **69b** Phantom Manor, © Disney; **70/71** Rustler Roundup Shootin' Gallery, © Disney; **71** Frontierland Disney, © Disney; **72** Adventureland logo, © Disney; **72/73** Adventureland bazaar entrance, © Disney; **74/75** Captain Hook's Gallery, © Disney; **75** Indiana Jones and the Temple of Peril, © Disney; **76** Pirates of the Caribbean, © Disney; **76/77** Pirates of the Caribbean, © Disney; **77** La Cabane de Robison, © Disney; **78** Fantasyland icon, © Disney; **78/79** The Enchanted Fairytale Ceremony, © Disney; **80** Alice's Curious Labyrinth, © Disney; **81** Kids go Free – Dumbo, © Disney; **82** It's a Small World, © Disney; **82/83** Mad Hatter's Tea Cups, © Disney; **84t** Sleeping Beauty's Castle, Fantasyland, © Disney; **84b** Sleeping Beauty's Castle, Fantasyland, © Disney; **85** Snow White and the Seven Dwarves, © Disney; **86t** Discoveryland logo, © Disney; **86/87** Space Mountain, Mission 2, © Disney; **87** Autopia, © Disney; **88/89** Orbitron, Machines, © Disney; **90/91** Space Mountain, © Disney; **91** Star Tours, © Disney; **92/93** The Legend of the Lion King Show, © Disney; **93** The Legend of the Lion King Show, © Disney; **94/95** Studio One entrance, © Disney; **95** Walt Disney Studios Logo, © Disney; **96t** Front Lot Logo, © Disney; **96b** Disney Studio 1 detail, © Disney; **97** Walt Disney Studio Stores Boutique, © Disney; **98t** Backlot icon, © Disney; **98b** Television Production tour, © Disney; **99** Moteurs Action! Stunt show spectacular, © Disney; **100** Animation Courtyard logo, © Disney; **100/101** Flying Carpets over Agrabah, © Disney; **101** Art of Disney Animation, © Disney; **102** Production Courtyard logo, © Disney; **102/103** Cyberspace Attraction, © Disney; **104/105** Domaine de Vaux-le-Vicomte, AA/B Rieger; **107** Chateau de Fontainebleau, AA/D Noble; **108** Chateau de Fontainbleau, Galerie de Diane, AA/D Noble; **109** Chateau de Vaux-le-Vicomte, AA/B Rieger; **110/111** Chateau de Versailles, Gardens, AA/M Jourdan; **112** Vincennes, AA/J A Tims; **113** Sealife Paris sign, © Disney; **114/115** Montmartre by night, AA/P Enticknap; **117t** Centre Georges Pompidou, AA/J A Tims; **117b** Centre Georges Pompidou, AA/C Sawyer; **118** View along Champs Elysees to Arc de Triomphe, AA/K Paterson; **118/119** Glass pyramid of the Louvre, AA/M Jourdan; **119** Jardin du Luxembourg, AA/M Jourdan; **120t** Le Marais, café scene, AA/M Jourdan; **120b** Watercolour artist, Montmartre, AA/P Enticknap; **121** Sacre Coeur, AA/A Souter; **122** Cathedrale de Notre Dame, AA/C Sawyer; **122/123** Notre Dame, AA/A Souter; **124/125** Eiffel Tower, AA/B Rieger

Every effort has been made to trace the copyright holders, and we apologise in advance for any unintentional omissions or errors. We would be pleased to apply any corrections in any following edition of this publication.